This beautiful prose collection strikes very deep notes. Rachel Hadas, known for her formal dexterity and intelligence, demonstrates here a remarkable fluency in moving from the disarmingly personal to the perceptively literary-critical, from the daily round to the ancient world, and from heartbreak to wonderment. Poetry is alive in her, as is a calm, humane attentiveness to the normalcy of grief and the possibilities of consolation.

PHILLIP LOPATE

In *Talking to The Dead*, Rachel Hadas' extraordinary new collection of essays, the author's voice comes through as that of a lifelong friend: compassionate, intelligent, completely understanding, often wickedly funny. A poet and a classicist, Hadas' acute perceptions are informed by a life of meticulous scholarship and deepened by personal experience. Here, among other explorations, she looks to Lucretius for an understanding of the devastation of Hurricane Irene, and seeks communion with her long-dead father, classical scholar Moses Hadas, "the demanding ghost." She visits her husband George, dying of early Alzheimer's disease in a residential facility, and sees him as separate from the world in the way of a nun who has "taken a veil." There is no veil for Rachel Hadas. Her vision is mercilessly, courageously clear and her writing, again in this book, is piercingly beautiful.

REEVE LINDBERGH

As I read *Talking to the Dead*, I felt I was engaged in a wide-ranging, personal, pleasurable, and erudite conversation with Rachel Hadas herself. She is deft, as few others are, at integrating her deep scholarship with a compassionate understanding of the human and the humorous everyday, and as she turns her sharp eye, clear intelligence, and ready wit on subjects as various as Dante and dreams, Homer and Plath, snakes and centaurs, illness and invisibility, she never fails to surprise, stimulate, and satisfy both heart and mind.

LYDIA DAVIS

Rachel Hadas not only speaks to her dead here, the public dead of literature, the private dead of family and friends (spheres that sometimes overlap), but listens to them, intently and affectionately. These are conversations, and the dead are as apt to pipe up as to be addressed, their own voices chiming in about poetry, criticism, teaching, and time. No one writes better than Hadas about what reading does, what reading is—an attic space between worlds, through which all worlds are accessible. In a phrase from Virgil that shows up again and again (a revenant itself) in these pages—quisque suos patimur manes—Hadas reminds us that we all have our own ghosts to bear. That said, we don't have to bear the past alone. Reading (and writing) is solitude, but also, paradoxically, companionship. And it is hard to imagine a better companion, erudite, unpretentious, relentlessly curious, funny, sharp, clear-eyed, always making unlikely but illuminating connections, than Hadas, on this enriching journey among the humane and literate shades.

A. E. STALLINGS

In this exploration of past and present, dream life and memory, Rachel Hadas illuminates the nature of poetry, family, love and friendship. Talking to the Dead demonstrates that a writer's life is inseparable from the life of her mind. We are fortunate indeed to have this collection of essays, memoirs, and entertainments from one of our best poets.

CHARLES MARTIN

The many voices in Rachel Hadas' *Talking to the Dead* include Dante, Homer, Cavafy, Plath, her father Moses Hadas, her late husband the composer George Edwards, the poet Alan Ansen, and neighbors in Vermont and Greece, to name only some of the appearances and geographies in these vividly engaged conversations with the not-so-dead of Hadas' cosmology. Brocades of the literary and lived speak for the rewards of a lifetime in letters. Whether the conversation is with Eliot as he argues with Milton's *Lycidas*, or her imaginings of Charles Dickens' reaction to a Semiotics course, a fantastic round table on the role of the humanities, we are ever in the presence of Hadas' gifts for showing us how "the words are there" to feed, guide, and teach us "in the realm of the invisible" where our ghosts are more alive than absent.

ADRIANNE KALFOPOULOU

Talking to the Dead is the best sort of criticism; a book that combines deep intellect and knowledge with genuine emotional power. Like Rachel Hadas's earlier memoir, Strange Relation, Talking to the Dead is a work of urgent scholarship, where the stakes are high, aesthetic questions matter, antiquity is relevant, and poetry provides both beauty and solace in individual lives.

FRANK HUYLER

TALKING TO
THE DEAD
Rachel Hadas

SPUYTEN DUYVIL
New York City

Copyright ©2015 Rachel Hadas
ISBN 978-1-941550-28-1
Cover art:

Library of Congress Cataloging-in-Publication Data

Hadas, Rachel.
 [Prose works. Selections]
 Talking to the dead / Rachel Hadas.
    pages ; cm
 ISBN 978-1-941550-28-1
 I. Title.
 PS3558.A3116A6 2015
 818'.54--dc23

                          2014034400

Table of Contents

THE GORGON'S GAZE

On Maundy Thursday, the night before Good Friday, it has been customary for the past twenty years or so for a number of poets and an audience of poetry lovers to gather in the Cathedral of Saint John the Divine on New York's Upper West Side to read Dante's *Inferno* aloud or to hear it read. The practice used to be to read all 33 cantos, which meant that the reading, which began about 9 PM, went on until well after midnight. But in recent years only selected cantos or passages from cantos have been read, so that the audience can get home before the small hours from what many evidently still find a threatening neighborhood. Poets and others who are invited by the Cathedral's Poet in Residence to be the readers express their preferences for which portions they want to read; they may or may not get their first choice, but are always free to choose the translation they prefer. A few read in Italian.

Each year's Dante reading is both similar to last year's and different from it. Of course the date, even the season, or what feels like the season, isn't constant. Sometimes Maundy Thursday falls in mid or late March, sometimes in early to late April. The weather may be balmy or uncertain or frigid. The participants also vary from one year to the next. People who read last year may not be in town this year or they may no longer be on earth. Armand Schwerner is one poet who comes to mind who is no longer among us; Rachel Wetzsteon, who didn't turn up to read in the spring of 2009 even though she had agreed to be there, has departed more recently. Some poets seem not to appear in public any more. Newcomers sometimes arrive, out-of-town poets who never turn up again. And so it goes. Still, despite all the coming and going, there's a fairly stable core of readers.

Each year, then, some twenty readers, mostly local poets, are invited to read. Some have translated Dante: Robert Pinsky, Michael Palma, Robert and Jean Hollander. Late in his life, James Merrill advised me, when I consulted him as to which rendering to read, to try Longfellow, whose beautiful translation I hadn't known. "Why didn't she read from mine?" a puzzled Pinsky (whose *Inferno* was newly out about then) asked someone or other.

The acoustics in the cavernous Cathedral are odd and unreliable. After a fire late in 2001, much of the interior space was reconstructed and renovated, and Poets' Corner events were temporarily moved further to the rear of the building; but each corner of the Cathedral has its own echoes and dead spots. There are microphones, which are needed; but voices can boom out, over-resonant and setting up ghostly reverberations, or can get lost in hissing whispers. It helps, though, that many people who attend the event bring their own texts in the original Italian or the translation of their choice and follow along in the book.

The sameness and changeability of the Dante reading from year to year recall the observance of any holiday or festival with its annual traditions and variations. Most salient is the association of Maundy Thursday with Good Friday, the climax of the Lenten lead-up to Easter Sunday, a feast compounded of darkness and light. It seems suitable that Easter weather in New York can veer from balmy breezes to blizzards, so that daffodils, tulips, and forsythia already blossoming in the parks can be covered by a blanket of white from which they boldly peek out, or which can melt the next day. The paschal zigzag from hope to despair and back is accentuated not only by the variability of the weather but by the contrast between the cold and dark outside the Cathedral and the cozily huddled audience inside.

After the reading, there's usually an organ interlude. There also used to be a reception at which deviled eggs and devil's food cake were served before we all trailed out into the night. I remember—this would have been around 2008—crossing Amsterdam Avenue with Tree Swenson, whose husband Liam Rector had shot himself at the end of the previous summer. She and I looked up at the full moon as we walked. Our talk was not about Liam, nor about my husband, ill with Alzheimer's, whom I had institutionalized a few months earlier, but about how the silvery moonlight reminded us of the country—Vermont in my case, the Pacific Northwest in hers.

Within the framework of the annual Dante reading, it is not only the date, the weather, and the particular readers and the passages they choose that vary from one year to the next. As always happens when we make a space for any enduring work of art, there is another variable too. What in Dante's journey, which detail of his durably vivid vision, will touch a listener's heart, resonate in his memory, or hook into her soul this time around? I can only speak for myself — although I intend also to let one other person, a friend who recently accompanied me to one of these evenings, speak as well. But I have no doubt that everyone who participates in or listens to this annual reading experiences the text differently each time. What grief, appetite, quirk, temptation, resentment, or episode in our past year's (or past life's) experience will find its reflection in some segment of the journey Dante so thrillingly traces for us? I was going to write "so unforgettably," but the truth is more complicated and interesting than that. We forget so much—so much even of our own lives, so much even of texts we think we know and cherish. One more function of this annual reading, then, is to help us to remember.

One year, as I recall (maybe more than one), the Virtuous Pagans spoke to me most clearly. I had been assigned to read the passage in Canto IV where Dante and Vergil encounter Homer, Horace, Ovid, and Lucan. Even in death, these figures embody culture in general and poetry in particular as a discourse spanning time and defeating death; their conversation leaps over petty obstacles like Christian faith. I especially loved the way the poets admit Dante to their company and talk to him — about what we are not to be told.

When they had talked together for a while,
        they turned to me with a nod of salutation,
        at which I saw my master broadly smile.
And then they made far greater demonstration
        of honor, bringing me up to their height,
        making me sixth in their wisdom's congregation.
So we walked onward, moving toward the light,
        and the things that were said among us it is good
        not to say here, as to say them there was right.

           (Canto IV, 97-105, tr. Michael Palma)

Another year, though, annoyed by the mannerisms of Reader A or frustrated by the inaudibility of Reader B, and myself assigned some other portion to read and therefore thinking more about that, I missed this poetic conversation entirely. But coming round dependably each spring, the Dante reading offers a fresh chance to pay attention.

Another passage to which I was often drawn, as many others surely were too, concerns not so much the continuity of human culture as the consistency of human nature. Though of course literature also plays a crucial role in the story of Paolo and Francesca's fateful reading session as narrated by Francesca in Canto V.

Some of the things we read made our eyes stray
        to one another's and the color flee
        our faces, but one point swept us away.
We read how that smile desired so ardently
        was kissed by such a lover, one so fine,
        and this one, who will never part from me,
trembling all over pressed his mouth on mine.

The book was a Gallehault, the author as well.
That day we did not read another line.

(Canto V, 133-138, tr. Michael Palma)

This beautiful vignette of reading together and what
may follow evokes a different scene for each reader or
listener. For me, it brought back 1970 in Alan Ansen's tall
old apartment on Alopekis Street in Kolonaki, in Athens.
Books definitely furnished the room; Alan's bookcases
were filled to bursting. On the tables stood vases filled
with drooping flowers whose murky water badly needed
changing. Alan and I read a lot of Dante together that
winter and early spring. We had our *quel giorno piu*
moment, a fleeting memory now; the subsequent decades
of our friendship easily survived that brief, odd liaison.
For Valentine's Day that year, I gave Alan as a valentine a
watercolor I'd painted of a heart mapped with routes and
figures, inscribing it "Hell is where the heart is." He had
my little painting framed and hung over his bed. I wonder
who owns it now.

Alan's and my interludes of reading were anything but
hellish. "There is no greater woe," says Francesca, "than
looking back on happiness in days/Of misery." But some
memories are very sweet. We got as far as somewhere in
Purgatory (I remember making a drawing of a procession
Dante describes, in an effort to visualize it) and then I left
town and the sessions came to an end.

Reader response is a starchy term for a process at
once natural, inevitable, individual, and potentially very

emotional. All readers respond to texts, and we all do so in our own way. Multiply my own few memories evoked by re-hearing bits of the *Inferno*—I've included only a couple of them—by the number of listeners, the people (poets, scholars, students, fans, tourists, passers-by) who come faithfully, or irregularly and serendipitously, to hear Dante and Vergil's passage through Hell performed again each spring. All of us readers and listeners are ourselves pilgrims of a sort. Inevitably, if we are paying attention at all we will recognize in some feature of the infernal landscape, some personage encountered on the journey, a part of our own lives.

Maybe some of the listeners are reminded of something in their own experience by the mud-bespattered gluttons, in Canto VI, or by the joyless souls in Canto VII:

> Set in the slime, they say: "We were sullen, with
>   no pleasure in the sweet, sun-gladdened air,
>   carrying in our souls the fumes of sloth.

> (Canto VII, 121-123, tr. Michael Palma)

Or maybe the flaming tombs of the heretics or the gleefully profane demons in the Bolgie seem especially eloquent. Maybe listeners are moved by the wood of the suicides, or by the courage Dante derives from hearing the mention of his beloved Beatrice's name. It's hard to say what makes one passage fly out to meet us, grabbing the drowsiest attention, while another disappears without a trace. Since this is an annual event, perhaps regular listeners respond most readily to what they recognize, remember, expect. Or perhaps beauty and power are trumped by familiarity, even though it is precisely our familiarity with a passage that makes us listen for it. Part of the mystery of reader response is that there is never any telling what that response will be. A familiar passage can feel stale, and something you've never paid attention to before can pounce on you out of nowhere.

An *Inferno* reading I remember unusually well took place on April 1, 1999 (that year Maundy Thursday fell on April Fool's Day). I don't remember which passage I was assigned to read, probably something pretty early in the canticle. I usually liked to get my reading over with early in case I wanted to go home before the end. In those days, I think, the practice was still to read the entire *Inferno* aloud, so by the time we arrived at Canto IX, it was getting fairly late. Vaguely planning to get home before midnight and waiting for a break so I could slip out (not an uncommon practice at these events), I was at the same time reluctant to leave.

I wasn't paying especially close attention to the portions of the poem after the first, familiar seven cantos. But at some point I realized that I was hearing something new. These were lines I had certainly read more than once before, and had probably also heard read aloud before at some earlier *Inferno* evening. But this time (and I have no recollection who was doing the reading— he or she must at least have been audible and clear), they reached my ear with sudden and complete authority and relevance. I recognized them as not only beautiful but true, or beautiful because true, in the blend of impatience and tenderness that they masterfully depicted.

I forget which translation I heard that night. But here is the relevant passage in Michael Palma's version. The Erinyes or Furies are harrying Dante, who is cowering close to his master for protection. Jeering, they threaten him with an even worse horror, the Gorgon Medusa, whose gaze turns people to stone.

> "Now let Medusa come! He'll be stone cold
>   when she gets done!" they cried. "It was a poor
>   revenge we took when Theseus was so bold!
> "Turn round and keep your eyes shut tight! Be sure
>   that if the Gorgon shows herself to you
>   and you look at her, you will see the world no more!"
> So my master cried, and with his own hands too
>   he covered my eyes when he had turned me round,
>   as if not trusting what my hands could do.

> (Canto IX, lines 52-60, tr. Michael Palma)

I was struck then, and am still struck now, thinking about the passage again more than a decade later, by the way Dante's loving and solicitous guide immediately *enacts* his own advice. He spins Dante bodily around and then, just to be sure, covers Dante's (already closed?) eyes with either hand. As I envision the scene, Vergil is standing behind Dante, engaging in what is less an embrace than a sort of friendly grappling. The posture, the body language, the intention—all strike me as quintessentially parental and above all maternal.

"Love must be put into action!" cries the old hermit in Elizabeth Bishop's enigmatic poem "Chemin de Fer." It is never clear what the eponymously solitary Hermit means by love, though one clue might be that earlier in the poem we are told that "The ties were too close together/Or maybe too far apart." However hermetic it is, the Bishop line comes to mind because I can hardly think of a better example of love in action than Vergil's action vis à vis Dante here. First he warns Dante, then prophylactically hugs him, covering Dante's eyes in the process. Words are necessary but not sufficient. Protection, prevention, coercion, affection, possessiveness, terror, impatience, impulse—all these emotions in a volatile and deeply human blend are somehow captured simultaneously, piled up on one another in this overdetermined embrace.

Dante is shielded by his master's arms for the time being, perhaps because he cannot be truly trusted to fend for himself at this perilous juncture. He may still (Vergil fears, so we do too) recklessly attempt to glimpse the Gorgon's face. But his master can't protect him forever. Sooner or later, and in the swift pace of this narrative, it is inevitably sooner, Vergil has to loosen his embrace and let Dante go. In fact, he does so only ten lines later, appropriately enough in order to encourage his charge to pay attention to something new:

My master said, removing the hands still pressed
     around my eyes: "Point the beam of your sight beyond,
     where the fumes from this ancient scum are bitterest."

         (Canto IX, lines 72-75, tr. Michael Palma)

And so straight on, at a characteristically tireless pace, to the next episode. When parental protection succeeds, as Vergil's does here, we feel free to ignore the past danger and move on.

One reason I was so struck by this episode in Canto IX is that my son was fifteen at the time, and was often out late at night with his friends. Our desire to shield the people whom we love most and who are most vulnerable, our children, is limitless; our power to protect them is very limited. My poem "The Red Hat," written about five years before that Maundy Thursday in 1999, speaks to just this pull, as the parents watch their child walking to school alone for the first time:

> He goes alone from there. The watcher's heart
> stretches, elastic in its love and fear,
> toward him as we watch him disappear,
> striding briskly.

The scene where Vergil covers Dante's eyes is sufficient proof that Dante understood such feelings perfectly well.

When I left the Cathedral that April Fool's night, I remember that spring had advanced far enough so that the forsythia were blooming, shining yellow in the lamplight—or was it the moonlight? It was my fifteen-year-old son's spring vacation, and he was with friends at Maxwell's in Hoboken, listening to jazz. I got home and settled in to wait. Where was my husband in all this? In 1999, his illness was not yet obvious, but he was already disengaging from the family, unable to remember details, sleeping a great deal. In effect, I was the single parent of an adolescent. Perhaps the passage in Dante had such resonance for me because Vergil functions as a single parent too.

An entire book could be written—very likely has already been—about individual responses to particular passages in Dante. Such a book could be classified as Dante Studies or as literary theory (reader response); it would fit both categories. If we think of the unforgettable chapter "The Ulysses Canto" in Primo Levi's Auschwitz memoir *If This is a Man*, Levi's recall of and response to the Ulysses episode in Canto XXVI, then the category of Holocaust Studies would need to be added. There is no limit to the ripples that emanate from this text.

I'll close with a ripple that is near and dear to me. In 2007, my friend and former student Keith O'Shaughnessy accompanied me to the Dante reading. At dinner beforehand, I gave Keith a small framed etching of Dante which had been given to me by Peter Hooten, the final partner of an earlier friend of mine, the poet James Merrill. I had kept this portrait but never put it on display; I always felt it belonged properly to someone else, not me. Keith was not only an ardent reader of Dante; he was also a fan of Merrill's poetry, and had even, as a student at Lawrenceville, heard Merrill read at the school, also the poet's alma mater.

The poem Keith later wrote about this *Inferno* evening, *Il Mio Tesoretto*, does several things at once. He memorializes our evening together and my passing on the gift of the Dante portrait to him; he recalls Merrill's Lawrenceville reading to an uncomprehending adolescent audience; he creates a chain of poetic tradition exemplified both by the passing on of the portrait and the familiarity of each younger poet with the older ones; he memorializes the event, the reading, itself; and he makes superbly graphic use of Dante's terza rima scheme, both in a homage to Dante and as a schematic way of braiding several strands together while constantly moving forward. Finally, as I have been arguing any listener or reader of the *Inferno* does, Keith seizes upon a particular character and episode which become iconic. Brunetto Latini, poetic tradition, a relay race: pass it on.

Il Mio Tesoretto
At an annual reading of Dante's *Inferno*

Just a bit more than midway through my life's journey,
I find myself raising Cain at the Cathedral
Of Saint John the Divine. It is Maundy Thursday—

Or Hallow's Eve for fans of the Infernal.
When I was just a bit less than a quarter
Way though the same hellish pilgrimage, an aging James Merill

(Alumnus of my high school) stood like an immortal,
Limbo-bent, before a room of sighing adolescents,
And taught them how a man makes himself eternal.

Now, as if to mingle breath with incense,
I mutter with the cantor, Ah, *Ser Brunetto*,
Are you *here*? and make tactile his winded spirit's omnipresence

Through a shade as ethereal as that patrician ghost's.
One reader finishes. Another adjusts her glasses,
Declaims a Medievalist's Florentine. At my elbow

Sits my own *miglior fabbro*, Rachel Hadas,
For whom my alma mater's James was simply Jimmy;
Under her chair, wrapped in plastic shopping bags,

Lies a tiny, wood-framed portrait of Sr. Alighieri
She tells me belonged to him. When at last that *maestro* moored
His lithe craft along the verge we make out so dimly,

His companion found it sitting in a drawer,
And passed it on to her, who took it home
And, as if gliding back from the same murky shore,

Buried the little treasure in a chest of her own.
At midnight, she, in turn, will pass it on
To me, who will carry it, through the Dis' divinely comic
                                        underground—

By subway, ferry, rail—further down, like the baton
At Verona, where the green cloth waves at the foot of the stair
To flickering stars, and the last man in, panting for Marathon,

Crows like the damned at blank space, through dead air,
To proclaim himself, if not the winner, there. [1]

---

1 Published in Keith O'Shaughnessy's *The Devil's Party* (Grolier Press, Fall 2014).

SYLVIA PLATH INTO GREEK

In 1973, I had been living on the island of Samos for more than two years, and I spoke the language (with a strong local accent) fluently enough for people to say, whether teasingly, admiringly, encouragingly, or even a bit threateningly I was never sure, "You'll forget English!" Not too likely; among the books I was rereading were *Persuasion, Middlemarch*, and *The Prelude*. There were also some slim volumes of Sylvia Plath's poetry that I'd ordered from Blackwells. My everyday conversations about okra and olive oil, neighbors and the weather, barely strayed indoors, let alone into the library in my head.

What was I thinking when it occurred to me around this time that I should take a stab at translating some poetry, even a single poem, into Greek? Not out of Greek into English—that idea, which made more sense, was to come later. My notion of translating a poem I liked into the daily idiom of our port, Ormos Marathakampou, was something like an attempt to reconcile the silent, invisible, reading side of my experience, a side steeped in English, with the public Greek-speaking side. Not that I ever imagined an audience for any translation I might produce; this was a feat undertaken for its own sake.

I chose Plath's "Poppies in July" for my short-lived project. Though not necessarily my favorite, this was one among many haunting poems in *Ariel*, one of my precious store of books. The volume I owned then has since disappeared, but I remember it perfectly: a small Faber paperback, dog-eared, stained with salt water or olive oil or coffee or just time, with "Rachel Kondylis" (my married name at the time) written on the flyleaf. Our little house was very close to the Aegean, and over the years the book acquired a strong flavor of mildew, which I can smell as I think about it now.

"Poppies in July" is short, direct, and relatively simple, with plenty of Plath's signature animus but a reasonably manageable vocabulary—after all, didn't poppies grow right outside our house? "Little poppies, little hell flames, / Do you do no harm?" The first stanza showed me that things weren't so easy. I was defeated by the second line, which I couldn't see any way to render (those two *dos*) without being hopelessly periphrastic. Do you really do no harm? Is it true that you do no harm? Both these options seemed awkward and wordy. The third and fourth stanzas were more amenable; I especially enjoyed "Like the skin of a mouth. // A mouth just bloodied. / Little bloody skirts!" Still, some challenge, whether it was the "nauseous capsules" or "your liquors seep to me," stopped me from pressing on to the end of the poem. I silently put my abortive translation aside.

Perhaps it was in reaction to this failure that I decided

to attempt my own poem in Greek, a project destined to be even more abruptly abandoned. Often my poems, like many people's, begin by scanning the scene before moving away in some other direction. And the scenery in Ormos was spectacular: the single sundrenched street, the big grey granite mountain to the west, to the south the sea. The quay where the fishing boats tied up was the centre of activity in what (in a poem written in English) I called the harbor frieze.

The Greek lines I produced may have been a composite record of sights I actually saw on the quay: "*Phortoma gaidouria kai karpouzia; / Phtasane ta caikia apo ta nisia.*" Translated, they read "Cargo of donkeys and watermelons! / The fishing boats have arrived from the islands." *Gaidouria, karpouzia* (or *karpouza*, as they say in Samos), *caikia*, and *nisia* (or *nisa*): alas, my two lines were no more than a bulging container for these four juicy neuter plurals. I failed to move beyond this embryonic grammar; I had no more to say. The poem ended right there, though the evocation of those round, glossy watermelons bouncing in the hull, and a donkey (can this be right?) being hoisted on to the *limani* in a sling, can still bring back those long summer days bathed in brilliant light.

However beautiful their backdrop, poems come above all from other poems, poems in the writer's mother tongue which he or she has read or otherwise absorbed. When I was living in Samos, no Greek poems were ringing in my ears. What decidedly filled my head was the daily conversation of my Ormos neighbors. The mysterious process by which one becomes even somewhat fluent in a new language is so absorbing that for a while it crowds out any doubts as to whether the subjects of conversation in the new tongue are all that interesting. If I was going to talk to my neighbors, then whatever we talked about would have to interest me. Anne Elliot in *Persuasion*, contemplating the prospect of a two- month visit to the very different social world of her sister and brother-in-law, has the attitude of a model student about to plunge into a language immersion course:

> She acknowledged it to be very fitting, that every little social commonwealth should dictate its own matters of discourse, and hoped, ere long, to become a not unworthy member of the one she was now transplanted into.

I was so busy taking in new words that the deliberate pace of the little social commonwealth in which I found myself was a relief. Formulaic snatches of talk, fillers, ostensibly the easy part of a language to learn, choreograph part of the etiquette of a village day. For example, it's only polite to acknowledge people each time you see them, even though you may run into the same person four or five times daily. Begin with *kali mera*, assuming it's morning; then downgrade to *kheretai* ("greetings") or simply *ya* ("health," but in effect "hi"). After the afternoon siesta, switch over to *kali spera* and repeat the sequence as needed, ending with *kali nikta* for the final encounter.

The heft and perennial freshness of these words is as hard to convey as the intensely social, public nature of the encounters they mark. The two lines of my abandoned poem only make any kind of sense in the context of a conversation with another housewife on the street; "the caique has come in, go check out the watermelons, and they're unloading donkeys too," or words to that effect.

In a good poem, nothing is ordinary. Whereas, in a new language, any word is an attention-getter, poems in our old language have to work to make us freshly aware of words or ideas worn thin, sometimes invisible, by use. One way of accomplishing this transformation from familiar to arresting is to use tropes; Plath's poppies as little bloody skirts or papery lips are a case in point.

If I'd somehow found a way of hearing Plath's voice speaking on Poseidon Street, in Ormos, if the vivid poppies had belonged to the same world as the donkeys and watermelons, then I might have been able to push through to the end of my translation. But even if I had found the precise dictionary meaning for every word in Plath's poem, the world of "Poppies in July"—what Anne Elliot might call the speaker's imagination, memory and ideas—had little to do with the sunlit gregariousness of the harbor.

TALKING TO MY FATHER

How to talk to the dead? The business bristles with obstacles. First of all, there's the difficulty of access: how to approach them or get them to approach you? In the *Odyssey*, the dead to whom Odysseus wishes to speak first have to taste sacrificial blood obtained under conditions strictly spelled out beforehand by Circe. Even Odysseus's mother licks the blood from his sword, an unsettling juxtaposition. Allegorical interpretations cluster around this high price paid for colloquy with shades.

Then there's the impossibility of touching the dead. Odysseus tries to embrace his mother:

> How I longed
> To embrace my mother's spirit, dead as she was!
> Three times I rushed toward her, desperate to hold her,
> three times she fluttered through my fingers, sifting away
> like a shadow, dissolving like a dream, and each time
> the grief cut to the heart, sharper, yes, and I,
> I cried out to her, words winging into the darkness:
> "Mother - why not wait for me? - How I long to hold you! -
> so even here, in the House of Death, we can fling
> our loving arms around each other, take some joy
> in the tears that numb the heart."

(*Odyssey* XI 233-45, tr. Robert Fagles)

In the *Aeneid*, Aeneas's father Anchises has been
eagerly awaiting the hero in the underworld:

> And when he saw Aeneas making toward him
> Over the grass, he stretched his hands out, blissful.
> The tears poured down his cheeks, and he exclaimed,
> "You've come at last? - love made you take this hard road,
> Just as I thought? - and can I see your face,
> My child, hear your beloved voice, and answer?
> Really, I counted on this, calculated
> The time, and anxious hope did not deceive me..."
> Aeneas answered, "Father, your sad image,
> Which often meets me, called me to this realm....
> My hand -
> Clasp it and don't retreat from my embrace."
> The tears poured down his face. Three times he tried
> To throw his arms around his father's neck,
> Three times the form slid from his useless hands,
> Like weightless wind or dreams that fly away.

> (*Aeneid* VI 685-91; 695-702 tr. Robert Fagles)

In a psychologically realistic paradox, the shades (one
thinks of Achilles, Agamemnon, even Dido) who are less
closely bound to the living visitor by ties of blood seem to
be less elusive, if only because the visitor to the House of
Death may not be so eager to embrace them.

A further difficulty is that the dead sometimes seem
more comfortable speaking to one another than to the
fleshly visitor. In the fourth Canto of the *Inferno*, Dante
is allowed to join Homer, Horace, Ovid, Lucan, and Vergil
in the circle of virtuous pagans, but we are not allowed
to hear the poets' conversation: "So we walked onward,
moving toward the light,/and the things that were said

among us it is good/not to say here, as to say them there was right." This is another kind of barrier to access; we get to hear what Francesca or Brunetto Latini say to Dante, but not what his fellow poets have to say. I'm reminded of being a little girl venturing in her nightgown to the top of the stairs in our Vermont house, listening to the grownups talking and laughing downstairs, wanting to join in the fun. But their words were not intended for me to hear. In order to join such conversations, we need to grow up.

Or maybe we need to die. The distinction blurs. Think of the denizens of the cemetery in *Our Town*, talking quietly to each other in the background. Or the grownups, barely audible on the bus, in Elizabeth Bishop's "The Moose," reminding the listener who hears fragments of their hushed talk of hearing, as a child, grownups talking in bed in another room: "In the creakings and noises,/an old conversation/—not concerning us, /but recognizable, somewhere,/back in the bus:/Grandparents' voices// uninterruptedly/talking, in Eternity...." That "in Eternity" leaps to prominence in the context of conversations among, if not with, the dead, conversations we strain to overhear.

A common way to try to access the kind of partially overheard conversations harking back to childhood Bishop is describing (though her reference to eternity provides a ghostly tinge) is to compare notes with someone else who was there and might remember, say pooling information with a sibling. In this connection, maybe it's significant that both Odysseus and Aeneas are only children with no such means of comparison. Dante too feels like a distinctly solitary character; there's no one among the living with whom he can debrief, except (a big except) the reader.

Even if one does have a sibling who might serve as a reality check, it's a truism that every child grows up in a different family, which is to say with a different perspective and different memories. Comparing notes a few years ago about our mother, who had died in 1992, my sister and I each remembered vividly a piece of worldly wisdom she had passed on to us when we were of college age. We were different people, and the advice we remembered was different. Our mother, a woman of measured, thoughtful and weighty utterances, had (perhaps repeatedly) admonished me: "Remember, honey, people are funny about money." To my sister, she had said "When you move into a new apartment, always bring light bulbs and soap." These pronouncements, both practical and somehow oracular, don't cancel each other out. But each does show a different side of their source.

Recovering the words of our dead is not only challenging but lonely. Whether the medium is a dream, a Ouija board, an archive of letters, or a meticulously researched reconstruction, the dead person who is gone and whom we seek to reconstruct, the silent person to whom we wish to restore speech, is not only fugitive, elusive, unhuggable. He or she, in whatever form we recover them, is individually tailored to us: our idiosyncratic recreation. Whether we're comparing notes about a parent with a sibling or trying to remember why we loved a certain teacher or friend, what we finally come up with is ours alone.

This loneliness is part of what the darkly luminous phrase from the sixth book of the *Aeneid—Quisque suos patimur manes*—means to me now. Anchises is explaining to his son on the latter's visit to the underworld what happens to souls after death. Here is how Sarah Ruden renders part of the passage:

> So souls are disciplined and pay the price
> Of old wrongdoing. Some are splayed, exposed
> To hollow winds; a flood submerges some,
> Washing out wickedness; fire scorches some pure.
> Each bears his own ghosts, then a few are sent
> To live in broad Elysium's happy fields,
> Till Time's great circle is completed...

(*Aeneid* VI 739-45)

Each bears his own ghosts. Ruden, whose translation of the Aeneid is virtually line for line, has managed to compress the four words of the Latin into only five English words. Here are a handful of strikingly different other ways this mysterious phrase has been rendered: "All have their Manes, and those Manes bear" (Dryden, 1697); "We all endure/Our ghostly retribution" (Christopher Pearse Cranch, 1872); "Each our own shade-correction we endure" (T.H. Delabere-May, 19th c.); "Each of us finds in the next world his own level" (Cecil Day Lewis, 1952); "First each of us must suffer his own shade" (Allen Mandelbaum, 1961); "Each of us must suffer his own demanding ghost" (Robert Fagles, 2006). In Ursula LeGuin's (2008) novel

Lavinia, which is based on the eponymous character in the *Aeneid*, the phrase is rendered "We each have to endure our own afterlife."

The ambiguities evident in this clutch of translations are pregnant and profound. There's always some sense of purgation, of punishment—Anchises is after all describing a process of judgment and purification. But there also seems to be a characteristically Vergilian introspection here, as if each of us has to live with his or her own individual legacy—not as a punishment but as a kind of lingering flavor of personality. What interests me is at least as much the *quisque* as the *Manes*. We each have to bear (or suffer, experience, endure) our own dead, including, after our deaths, ourselves. I may be straying from the Latin's meaning, but the phrase seems to encompass in its four words not only the sense that after our deaths we each undergo an individually tailored process of purification, but also that we experience the death of anyone we care about differently from the way anyone else will experience that death.

It seems fitting that I've scooped these words from their context in a lecture Anchises is delivering. Aeneas has asked him "Father, do some souls really soar back skyward/From here, returning into sluggish bodies?/ What dreadful longing sends them toward the light?" The entire answer is magnificent, but somehow the four words *Quisque suos patimur manes* went straight to my heart, as they evidently went straight to LeGuin's. And if I'd been Aeneas, listening to his father's expatiation, I think these would have been the words that stayed with me.

For the paradoxical fact is that less can often mean more. Light bulbs and soap; people are funny about money—easy to remember. The more of a record (especially a written record) our dead leave, the more we have to have recourse to cherry picking a significant word, a remembered remark—what Homer calls a *kledon* (according to Cunliffe's *Lexicon of the Homeric Dialect*, "an omen or presage, something said which bears a significance of which the speaker is unconscious, a speech that serves as an omen"). James Merrill, writing about Cavafy, mentions "those moments familiar to us all when the stranger's idle word or the friend's sudden presence happens to strike deeply into our spirits." The stranger or the friend, though, are not our beloved dead, and theirs are words we don't have to dig for. If the deceased person with whom we long to converse has left an abundant written record, maybe a semi-aleatory method works best, a lazy kind of *sortes vergilianae*: let chance determine which phrase jumps out.

What I'm circling here is the most recent of my periodic impulses to commune with the *manes* of my father, Moses Hadas (1900-1966). The obstacles to any such colloquy turn out to be more numerous than the heads of Cerberus. I was seventeen when Moses died. A self-absorbed adolescent, therefore, I missed one opportunity after another in his last years to ask him, while it was still possible for us to talk, about his past: family, education, career, war, even such adventures as a trip to Israel with Eric Sevareid to tape a TV feature on the Shrine of the Book. Nor was my father particularly forthcoming as a personality. He had a reticence I think I recognize in myself—a reticence complicated by a quality of adaptability I fumblingly touched upon in "The Many Lives of Moses Hadas," a piece I wrote for Columbia Magazine in 2000:

> His work as teacher and scholar was a constant, but this work was performed by, at different times, an Orthodox Jew and—as he once described himself to some proselytizing Jehovah's Witnesses—a godless person... He was a Southerner by upbringing and accent, then a New Yorker. He was a rabbi, then a professor, then, like many academics of his generation, an O.S.S. operative who, more unusually, took an active interest in Greek politics after the war, and then a professor again, not to mention a talking head on TV and a tele-lecturer. He was a scholar at home in three ancient languages who was also a Groucho Marx fan. He was a husband and father to two very different families in succession....It's as if it were possible, just barely, to live all these lives, but only if no time was wasted talking about them. Or writing about them—for much of Hadas's personality, let alone his experience, remains outside the scope of his written work.

My half-brother David Hadas hints at both the reticence and the adaptability when he writes in his Foreword to a reprint of Moses' last book, *Fables of a Jewish Aesop*, "many people found him very Southern. When he wanted to, Moses could also seem very Jewish." David's own reticence here has a sidelong, charged eloquence I missed when I first read this little piece, which so far as I know was the only tribute to his father David, a reluctant writer, ever put on paper. I wish that David were still available to talk to about (among other things) Moses—how many questions I'd ask him! But David too has now joined the ranks of complicated shades accessible only through individual efforts. Ask David's colleagues, students, and children about him and you get (what else?) a mosaic.

So what kind of *manes* of my long departed father am I experiencing or bearing or suffering now? There are scattered snapshots of physical memories, freeze-frame glimpses. We used to lie side by side, on his and my mother's bed, reading Cicero's *De Senectute* when I was a junior in high school and he was too tired after a day's teaching to sit up. There are a few letters he wrote to me over the years, or rather my memories of those letters, which have themselves been swallowed up by time. There are a few things he said, or I think he said, to me. There's a late conversation sitting on a bench near Grant's Tomb. A final phone call. Increasingly, it seems to me, our exchanges were burdened or stretched thin by the gap of forty-eight years between our ages and a weight of weariness and preoccupation that he never talked about but that seems palpable to me now. But this cloud of mortality (for that is what it was) also pressed triviality out of our conversations. Much went unsaid—there were things that he knew I knew, and I think I knew he knew this—but nothing that I remember of what was said strikes me as trivial or evasive. Without naming either of them, he and I shared love and reticence.

Now that I am rapidly approaching the age at which my father died, it is to his writings I have to turn if I want to be addressed as an adult. Not that his books are addressed to me—but then poetry, which has always been my tutelary genre, isn't addressed to anyone in particular either. Written or spoken, an utterance—Homer's winged words—flies free of its occasion. I recently revisited my father's 1962 book *Old Wine New Bottles: A Humanist Teacher at Work*. As any significant book does, it had changed for me over time. Now myself a veteran of more than thirty years in the classroom, I was most interested in the passages about teaching. Sharon Olds used to remind her students to worry less about who they were speaking to than who they were speaking for—a useful piece of advice to bear in mind.

> I am a teacher, (*Old Wine New Bottles* begins.) ...I have written books and given public lectures, but these I have regarded as part of my teaching... what goes on in my own and a thousand other classrooms is more important than the large affairs carried on in the shining palaces of aluminum and glass downtown. For I believe that education is mankind's most important enterprise.

Yes! I thought. Nor is this just a rah-rah promotional statement. What underlies it is among other things a wistful acknowledgement of limits:

> The greatest advantage education can offer is that it enables a shortlived and time-bound individual to move in several cultural climates simultaneously...

Short-lived: my father wrote these words a few years before his death at sixty-six. Time-bound: a condition of our brief human lifespan. Several cultural climates simultaneously: as I wrote in "The Many Lives of Moses Hadas," my father was a multi-culturalist *avant la lettre*. He seldom writes directly about being Jewish, but his 1959 book *Hellenistic Culture: Fusion and Diffusion* is devoted to the fertile merging of different cultural traditions, which is a subtext as well of *Fables of a Jewish Aesop*. This posthumously published volume is doubly eloquent not only in its juxtaposition of "fables" and "Jewish," but in that the fables were translated by my father. In more than one way, his last book was a cross-over.

For of course one way to effect cultural transmission, to "enable a short-lived and time-bound individual" who is probably also linguistically challenged "to move in several cultural climates simultaneously," is translation. Moses' own lingering unease with even the notion of the kind of unscholarly popularization implied by the existence of classics in translation comes through clearly in more than one passage of *Old Wine New Bottles*. Whenever he mentions this issue, he comes closer than usual to unveiling his own mixed feelings. Characteristically, he also leaves something out.

> ...it has taken me many years to shed the feeling of guilt in working with translations, which many others could do as well, to the possible neglect of the things I had been trained to do. I did not finally shake the feeling off until all of my own teachers were retired, but I have continued with teaching translations and have gloried in it.

Omitted here is the fact that Moses proceeded (presumably once he had shed his burden of guilt), to do a great many translations himself; *Fables of a Jewish Aesop* was the last in a long series of translations from German, Greek, and Latin. Was this work accomplished "to the possible neglect of the things I had been trained to do?" The topic, plainly a troublesome one, arises again elsewhere in *Old Wine New Bottles*:

> Professional exclusiveness has happily been relaxed, but vestiges of it persist, as I can testify from personal experience. When I was invited, two or three years ago [that is, about 1959] to address a meeting of teachers on problems of teaching classics in translation, the distinguished scholar who introduced me informed the audience that I was a man who made translations, wrote popularizing interpretations, and even reviewed books in my field for newspapers; he plainly meant no unkindness, but just as plainly found it remarkable that the professor of Greek in a reputable university should stray so far from the traditional boundaries. About 1940, I published a study of the religion of Plutarch in a scholarly but nonclassical periodical, and was told by senior colleague, who was also a warm friend, that I had done very wrong not to publish it in a classical periodical. When I realized that he was in earnest, I said, "But the classicists already know; this will interest other people and should be made available to them." "Your responsibility is to your your own profession," my colleague said.

This issue of professional responsibility is one of many I wish I had raised with my father; one of many open questions to which I have to find answers in what he wrote. I also wonder whether he felt that his trip to Israel with Eric Sevareid, or his telephone lectures to black colleges, meant he was neglecting the things he had been trained to do. I imagine that as the years went by, Moses got used to this versatility. After all, as he wrote, "I have written books and given public lectures, but these I have regarded as part of my teaching." Still, there remains the sense of a busy, accomplished, and rather short life with no breathing space for a rest—a sense I feel more keenly (as I get older and more tired) that he himself felt—not that he ever mentioned it.

Another question I never thought to ask during my father's lifetime: was there any lingering feeling of guilt, not at working on translations, but at a more personal kind of transformation: leaving the Jewish community in which he had been raised, leaving his early career as a rabbi, leaving his first wife and their teenaged children? Religion is an issue Moses skirts in his more— his relatively—autobiographical work. When he uses the word "spiritual" in *Old Wine New Bottles,* it's generally in the context of his overt and abiding concern, education. For education and spirituality turn out to overlap. I enjoyed this tart sentence, which I'd missed on earlier readings:

> For most of the centuries of European history qualifying education as spiritual would be as tautological as calling water wet.

Finally, I had also missed this remarkable passage, which begins in the context of classical pedagogy but moves to deeper waters:

> To say that the classics were abolished from the curriculum by men who had studied them and then restored by men who had not is exaggeration, but it comes near enough truth to make the official guardians of the classical tradition uncomfortable. The sequence of ossification, revitalization, ossification, revitalization, is a phenomenon common to all spiritual concerns [among which, as we've seen, Moses includes education], and particularly noticeable in religion. Zeal tends to calcify into a rote ritualism, and is then revivified, to the chagrin and often against the opposition of the official priesthood, by a man from the desert who is not a member of the prophets' guild. The renewal, if it is effective, is then incorporated into the body of the tradition in charge of the priesthood, again hardens into spiritless routine, and again invites revivification at the hands of people who have no vested interests in the subject, to the discomfort of those who have.

Wasn't Moses himself, in his daring career as a classicist, "a man from the desert?" If so, then the members of the prophets' guild, those with a vested interest in the subject, the "clerkly teachers," as he calls them elsewhere, were surely his elders, his own teachers, the resisters of change, who had to retire before he could shed the feeling of guilt at being a translator and popularizer. Also implied, more subtly, is that this outlier from the desert also failed to join the prophets' guild because his allegiance, at least by birth and upbringing, was to another tribe.

This, then, is the demanding ghost to whom these days I find myself reaching out; the ghostly retribution I am enduring; the shade I am suffering. I open my arms to embrace Moses, and he slips away. But the words are there.

Pages of Illustrations

A Round-Table Discussion, Moderated by Rachel Hadas and featuring Edward Hirsch (*How to Read a Poem and Fall in Love with Poetry*); Mary Kinzie (*A Poet's Guide to Poetry*); Kenneth Koch (*Making Your Own Days: The Pleasures of Reading and Writing Poetry*), and Robert Pinsky (*The Sounds of Poetry: A Brief Guide*) with guest appearances by John Berryman, Tommaso Ceva, Michael Connelly, T.S. Eliot, E.M. Forster, Robert Frost, Robert Graves, Marianne Moore, Frank O'Hara, Boris Pasternak, Edgar Allan Poe, William Shakespeare, Wallace Stevens, Paul Valery, and Walt Whitman.

Hadas: Welcome, distinguished guests. Good evening, everybody. I'll start the ball rolling by playing devil's advocate: There are entirely too many new books about poetry! Molly Peacock and Timothy Steele just couldn't fit into tonight's program, and I'm sure there are others waiting in the wings. Either these books overlap, which is redundant; or they contradict one another, which is confusing. Sometimes they do both.

On the other hand, isn't it a sign of cultural

health that there should be so many books devoted to the art of poetry? If people are reading, or even just buying, *How to Read a Poem* or *Making Your Own Days*, then surely this indicates a desire to know more about poetry.

On the third hand, though, who would want to read the books if they didn't know something about poetry already—except maybe college students assigned to read them?

Yet these books wouldn't work very well as textbooks or handbooks. They approach their subject from too far away or too close up—is that the problem? Either the tone drips with awe, Ed, or, Mary, the style is both technical and obscure. Either way, no matter how hard the author tries to be either rhapsodic or else just brisk and factual, there's something off-putting about the tone of just about all these books. Of course as a poet and teacher, I'm impossibly jaded—I can't be the intended audience.

Pinsky: Excuse me, that's not fair to my *Guide*. I try to explain the principles in plain language, with a minimum of special terms, objectively, by paying close attention to particular poems and specific words. Technical language, vague impressions about the emotional effects of sounds (the supposedly exuberant or doleful *w*'s, the anxious or sensual *t*'s, etc.), elaborate systems, categories that need memorizing, little accent marks and special typographical symbols—all these, I work to avoid.[1]

Hadas: Fair enough. But your scruples didn't stop you from adding to this pile of books, did they?

Kinzie: I believe poets read poetry differently than non-poets do.[2]

Hadas: Isn't there a grammatical error there? Oh well, poets probably write prose differently than non-poets do too.

Koch: You're all going too fast. Your discussion assumes you know what poetry is, but no one really has any idea. Poetry is often regarded as a mystery, and in some respects it is one. No one is quite sure where poetry comes from, no one is quite sure exactly what it is, and no one knows, really, how anyone is able to write it. The Greeks thought, or at least said, that it came from the Muse, but in our time no one has been able to find her.[3]

Hadas: Except maybe Albert Brooks.

---

1 Robert Pinsky, *The Sounds of Poetry: A Brief Guide* (New York: Farrar, Straus & Giroux, 1998), 56.
2 Mary Kinzie, *A Poet's Guide to Poetry* (Chicago: University of Chicago Press, 1999), 1.
3 Kenneth Koch, *Making Your Own Days: The Pleasures of Reading and Writing Poetry* (New York: Touchstone, 1998), 19.

Hirsch: Kenneth, I must say I think your transparent
humility in the face of what you imply is
ineffable and unknowable is really insincere
obscurantist claptrap. No one is sure
what poetry is? I can offer you dozens of
multicultural, richly metaphorical, and deeply
inspirational definitions of poetry from the
whole span of human history. Shouldn't we start
with a few of those? My book is full of them.

Kinzie: I have some catchy definitions too. Here's one
you'll like: All poetry comes into being in respect
to its sounds, tormented into perfection or near-
perfection by the logical and prosaic resistance
of language in response to the disturbance of
occasion. [4]

Hadas: That poet's prose again—rolls right off the
tongue.

Koch: Run that by me again, please, Mary. It's a little
abstruse for a simple fellow like me. After all,
poetry, because it stirs such strong feelings and
because great examples of it are so rare, has often
been written about in ways that make it seem
more difficult, mysterious, more specialized,
and more remote than it actually is—it is written
about as a mystery, as a sort of intellectual/
aesthetic code that has to be broken, as an

4 Kinzie, 1.

example of some aspect of history or philosophy. Non-specialist readers are likely to find such writing more difficult to understand than poetry, and in fact not always on the subject of poetry, so it ends up being not much help.[5]

Cicero: May I comment from the audience? Speaking as one of those non-specialist readers, thank god, I say: "Intellectual/aesthetic code?" Balderdash! Even if my lifetime were to be doubled, I still wouldn't have time to waste on reading the lyric poets.[6]

Pinsky: But think how much more time you'd waste reading guidebooks—except my nice slim one, of course.

Hadas: Can we get back to definitions? What Ed pithily calls Cicero's hostile indifference to poetry, so characteristic of politicians,[7] just goes to show that there always have been and always will be depressed old Scrooges who are blind and deaf to beauty, who fail to respond to the most intimate and volatile form of literary discourse.[8] Did I get that right, Ed?

---

5 Koch, 13.
6 Edward Hirsch, *How to Read a Poem and Fall in Love with Poetry* (New York: Harcourt Brace, 1999), xii.
7 Hirsch, xii.
8 Hirsch, xi. , 9. Koch, 19.

Valery: May I speak? I have a less sentimental and hyperbolic definition: poetry is a language within a language.[9]

Hirsch: Poetry is a form of necessary speech![10]

Pinsky: Right. The hearing-knowledge we bring to a line of poetry is a knowledge of patterns in speech we have known to hear since we were infants. If we tried to learn such knowledge by elaborate rules or through brute, systematic memorization, we would not be able to use them as fluently as we do.[11]

Hirsch: I think you're taking "speech" too literally, Robert.

Koch: There's another point about poetry as speech: poetry is an odd sort of language in that everyone who uses it well changes it slightly, and this fact helps to explain poetic influence and how poetry does change from one time and one poet to another. If we take the idea of a poetic language seriously (thanks, Paul), it can be defined first as a language in which the sound of words is raised to an importance equal to that of their[12] meaning.

9   Koch, 19.
10   Hirsch, xii.
11   Pinsky, 5.
12   Koch, 20.

Pinsky: I agree with some of that. Every speaker, intuitively and accurately, courses gracefully through immensely subtle manipulations of sound. It is almost as if we sing to one another all day.[13]

Pasternak: If I may? Words and melody! Poetry searches for music amidst the tumult of the dictionary.[14]

Hirsch: The lyric poem walks a line between speaking and singing. [15]

Koch: It's hard to say if the music of poetry creates the emotion in a poem, or if it is the poem's emotion that creates the music. Probably both are true.[16]

Hadas: I'm confused. Poetry is a language within a language, it's music, it's a form of necessary speech, it's—

Ceva: Tommaso Ceva, Madame. A baroque Jesuit poet. Poetry is also a dream dreamed in the presence of reason.[17]

13 Pinsky, 3.
14 Koch, 27.
15 Hirsch, 10.
16 Koch, 27.
17 Hirsch, 27.

Hadas: Sounds like a Goya etching. Okay—but don't we
get a little lost amidst all these fancy definitions?
We're still quibbling about a single word.

Frost: Well, all the fun's in how you say a thing.[18]

Graves: In using the word Poetry I mean both the
controlled and uncontrollable parts of the art
taken together, because each is helpless without
the other one.[19]

Humpty-Dumpty: *(scornfully)* When I use a word,
it means just what I choose it to
mean—neither more nor less.[20]

Hadas: All these books about poetry, with their
elaborate definitions and disclaimers, have the
effect of making me want to read a poem, or
even a whole anthology—anything but poetic
prose about poetry.

Kinzie: Not all that poetic. Open my book anywhere.

Pinsky: Rachel is quite right. Art proceeds according
to principles discernible in works of art.
Therefore, if one is asked for a good book
about traditional metrics, a good answer is:

18 Robert Frost, "The Mountain," line 104.
19 Hirsch, 25.
20 Lewis Carroll, *Through the Looking Glass*, Chapter VI.

The Collected Poems of William Butler Yeats, or
The Complete Poems of Ben Jonson. Two excellent
books about so-called free verse are the two-
volume *Collected Poems of William Carlos Williams*
and *The Collected Poems of Wallace Stevens.* One of
the most instructive books on short lines is *The
Complete Poems of Emily Dickinson.* To learn a lot
about the adaptation of ballad meter to modern
poetry, an invaluable work is *Thomas Hardy:
The Complete Poems.* No instruction manual can
teach as much as careful attention to the sounds
in even one great poem.

But—ahem!—a guide can be helpful.[21]

Hadas: Somehow I saw that coming. I do like your guide,
which is clear and short and concentrates pretty
much on one aspect of poetry without too much
fussing about definitions.

Koch: I was guided by the same principles as Robert,
but I helpfully included a small anthology in my
book about poetry. Poems were chosen for the
anthology to exemplify and illuminate what is
said in the chapters. [22]

Hadas: I think that passive is a little shifty, Kenneth. But
let's see if I have this straight. Poems are chosen
(by whom, I wonder?) to illustrate principles?
Or—

21 Pinsky, 15.
22 Pinsky, 15.

Pinsky: Principles may be discerned in actual practice:
for example, in the way people actually speak,
or in the lines poets have written. [23]

Koch: You speak as if actual practice were monolithic.
I've already said this evening that poetry is an
odd sort of language in that everyone who uses it
well changes it slightly. A transfer takes place: by
reading, a young poet can possess what has taken
hundreds of years to develop. Poets "cut in" on
other poets and whirl partners away into their
own poems. They are able to pick up new steps
and do variations on them in what seems no time
at all. [24]

Hadas: I like your notion of poets cutting in on each
other—a sort of vast synchronic ballroom full of
dancers. Someone said that James Merrill was
the Fred Astaire of poetry.

Merrill: *...THE ROSEBRICK MANOR*
ALL TOPIARY FORMS & METRICAL MOAT
RIPPLING UNSOUNDED! FROM ANTHOLOGIZED
PERENNIALS TO HERB GARDEN OF CLICHES
FROM LATIN-LABELED HYBRIDS TO THE FAWN
4-LETTER FUNGI THAT ENRICH THE LAWN,
IS NOT ARCADIA TO DWELL AMONG
GREENWOOD PERSPECTIVES OF THE MOTHER

23 Pinsky, 7.
24 Koch, 20,71.

TONGUE....
AS FOR THE FAMILY ITSELF MY DEAR
JUST GAPE UP AT THAT CORONETED FRIEZE:
SWEET WILLIAMS & FATE-FLAVORED EMILIES
THE DOUBTING THOMAS & THE DULCET ONE
(HARDY MY BOY WHO ELSE? & CAMPION) [25]

Hirsch: I don't think I'm getting enough air time for my definitions. Here's one:

The poem is an act beyond paraphrase because it is always inseparable from the way it is being said.[26]

Stevens: Pages of illustrations.[27]

Koch: As I quote you saying on page 15 of my book.

Stevens: Mr. Hirsch quotes me on page 244 of his book: "Poetry is like prayer in that it is most effective in solitude and in times of solitude as, for example, in the earliest morning."[28]

O'Hara: I can dig that, depending on what you mean by early. Listen to the beginning of my poem "A True Account of Talking to the Sun at Fire Island:"

25 James Merrill, *Mirabell: Books of Number*, 9.1.
26 Hirsch, 10.
27 Wallace Stevens, "Connoisseur of Chaos," line 3.
28 Hirsch, 244.

> The Sun woke me this morning
> loud and clear, saying 'Hey! I've been
> trying to wake you up for fifteen
> minutes..."

Stevens: That is not exactly what I had in mind by
solitude, Mr. O'Hara.

Koch: I included that poem in my little anthology,
Frank. You only get to say it here because I like to
put poems by my friends in my books. My friends
are the best poets, of course.

O'Hara: "Talking to the Sun" is in plenty of other
anthologies too. I can say it all over the place,
despite the fact that I've been dead since 1966.

Hirsch: Q.E.D. The lyric poem seeks to mesmerize time.
It crosses frontiers and outwits the temporal.
It seeks to defy death, coming to disturb and
console you. [29]

Shakespeare: No, time, thou shalt not boast that I do
change.[30]

Berryman: These Songs are not meant to be understood,
you understand. They are only meant to

29 Hirsch, 5.
30 Shakespeare Sonnet 123, line 1.

terrify & comfort.[31] Were you quoting me,
Mr. Hirsch?

Hirsch: Of course. I credit you, too.

Berryman: Sorry, I've been too busy reading reviews of
my new posthumous book of Shakespeare
criticism. Us real poets don't have to
publish our critical prose until after we're dead.
You get more mileage that way.

Hadas: May we go back a little? I think I'm beginning
to understand. Guides to poetry are intended
to send us back to poetry, or maybe to send us
to poetry in the first place. We appreciate the
poems much more if we realize how perfectly
they illustrate the principles set forth in the
guides. Jimmy Merrill says of Ephraim that
like a perfect guide, he answers questions his
interlocutors had lacked the wit to ask. [32]

Hirsch: But Rachel is leaving out the dimension of awe
and wonder. We are instructed by Whitman in
the joy of starting out that the deepest spirit of
poetry is awe. Poetry is a way of inscribing that
feeling of awe.[33]

31 Hirsch, 5.
32 Merrill, *The Book of Ephraim*, Section C.
33 Hirsch, 3.

Whitman: (leaping to his feet and orating)

> Have you reckoned a thousand acres much? Have
> you reckoned the earth much?
> Have you practiced so long to learn to read?
> Have you felt so proud to get at the meaning of
> poems?
> Stop this day and night with me and you shall
> possess the origin of all poems.
> You shall possess the good of the earth and the
> sun... [34]

Hadas: Thanks, I'll take a rain check. Our time is almost up.

Frost: But I have promises to keep
And miles to go before I sleep. [35]

Hadas: You got it.

Hirsch: But the lyric left behind proposes a legacy
beyond death.[36]

Kinzie: Or to put it with my customary flair, the arts
provide medium of connection between people
in different periods.[37]

Hadas: Thank you, Mary. You know, I feel almost ready
to read a novel now.

34 Walt Whitman, *Leaves of Grass*, Section 2.
35 Frost, "Stopping by Woods on a Snowy Evening."
36 Hirsch, 155.
37 Kinzie, 173.

Moore: I too dislike it.[38]

Hadas: Novels?

Moore: Poetry.

Hotspur: I had rather be a kitten and cry mew
        Than one of these same meter ballad-
        mongers.[39]

Hadas: Thank you, my lord. Did I say synchronic?
        Anyway, I'm afraid we're just about out of time.

Poe: (hollowly) Out of space, out of time.[40]

Connelly: Say, Edgar, I used that quote in my novel *The
        Poet*, about a serial killer who hypnotized his
        victims, before murdering them, into writing
        a Poe quote into their suicide note. Quote/
        note! I'm a poet too.

Frost: All metaphor breaks down somewhere. That is
        the beauty of it. It's touch and go with metaphor,
        and until you have lived with it long enough you
        don't know when it is going. You don't know how
        much you can get out of it and when it will cease
        to yield.[41]

38 Marianne Moore, "Poetry," line 1.
39 Shakespeare, *Henry IV Part I*, Ill.i. 125-6.
40 Edgar Allan Poe, "Dream-Land."
41 Frost "Education by Poetry: A Meditative Monologue."

Connelly: Well, it yielded plenty for me. I bet a single one of my books sells dozens of times more copies than all these poetry guides put together. Don't get me wrong—I like poetry fine.

Moore: I too dislike it.

Hadas: Miss Moore, adjust your hearing aid. Mr. Connelly said he liked poetry.

Moore: *(muttering)* Imaginary gardens... real toads... [42]

Koch: As I keep saying, everyone who uses the poetry language changes it slightly.

Frost: Poetry is a way of saying one thing and meaning another. [43]

Shakespeare: For I have sworn thee fair, and thought thee bright,
Who art as black as hell, as dark as night. [44]

Hadas: But don't you also talk about belying your love with false compare, Mr. Shakespeare?[45] *(yawns)* Oh, it's getting really late.

---

42 Moore, "Poetry."
43 Frost.
44 Shakespeare Sonnet 147, lines 13-14.
45 Shakespeare Sonnet 130, line 14.

Keats: Ma'am, have you never heard of negative capability, that is, when man is capable of being in uncertainties, Mysteries, doubts, without any irritable reaching after fact or reason?[46]

Hirsch: I quote that, did you know? Page 131.

Hadas: I know why we can't seem to stop. Everybody wants to have the last word.
> *Poetic Closure*—where is Barbara Herrnstein Smith when we need her?
> No, no, forget I asked.

Hirsch: Didn't I say that the lyric poem outwits the temporal?

Hadas: Does that mean it has to go on forever?

Eliot: *HURRY UP PLEASE IT'S TIME*
HURRY UP PLEASE IT'S TIME [47]

Hadas: Goonight, Ed. Goonight, Robert. Goonight, Kenneth. Goonight, Mary.
Goonight, Wallace and Walter, Robert and Marianne, James and
William, Edgar and Paul. Who have I forgotten?
Cicero. Tommaso. Frank.
Thanks so much for joining us.[48]

---

46 Keats, Letter, December 12,1817.
47 T.S. Eliot, The Waste Land, lines 168-9.
48 Eliot, *The Waste Land*, 172; Shakespeare, *Hamlet*, IV. v. 73-4.

Goodnight, ladies, goodnight, sweet ladies,
Goodnight, goodnight. [49]

Goethe: *(spectrally)* In poetry, especially in that
which is unconscious, before which reason
and understanding fall short, and which,
therefore, produces effects so far surpassing all
conception, there is always something of the
Demoniacal.

Hirsch: I quoted you saying that. It counts as another
definition.

Hadas: Ed, Johann Wolfgang, thanks again.

BLACKOUT

---

49 Hirsch, 24.

Rachel Wetzsteon and Allusion

My friend and neighbor Rachel Wetzsteon, who died three years ago, recently made an unexpected and welcome reappearance in my life, in the form of an essay published in the new edition of the *Princeton Encyclopedia of Poetry and Poetics*. Appropriately, this learned poet and critic, whose doctoral dissertation at Columbia was later published as *Influential Ghosts: A Study of Auden's Sources*, had contributed the article on allusion. Rachel does a good job, classifying allusion in six categories: topical, personal, formal, metaphoric, imitative, and structural. As I read her brief but pithy article, I realized that for some months past I'd been compiling a private mental list of various kinds of verbal echoes that were all some kind of allusion.

The examples that stuck in my head blurred into one another, and were in some way elusive or otherwise problematic. They didn't correspond entirely to Rachel's categories. For example, an aphorism, gnomically uttered by my husband in his later years—"You can't have everything, but sometimes you can have nothing"—turned out to be a version of a saying attributed to the actress and politician Glenda Jackson, which I was surprised to come across the other day in one of those notebooks whose otherwise blank pages are illuminated by quotations from celebrities. "I used to believe that anything was better than nothing. Now I know that sometimes nothing is better," Jackson once said. But when? Where? One might call this phenomenon the untraceable allusion.

In her article, Rachel writes: "Allusion tends to assume an intelligent reader, a shared body of knowledge, and the value of previous works or contexts." This holds for the common-or-garden allusion. At a recent reading from the *Best American Poetry 2012* anthology, one poet addressed a sunflower, borrowing from Blake: "Weary of time? I think not." Another poet, in a poem called "Daffodil," used a line from Wordsworth to charmingly smirking effect in an epigraph: "A poet could not but be gay." The assumption is that we intelligent readers know Blake's "Ah, sunflower, weary of time" and Wordsworth's "A poet could not be but gay / In such a jocund company." Still, I wondered whether all or even most of the enthusiastic young people packing the New School auditorium did know the original poems. (Strangely, it didn't seem to matter.)

A furtive cousin of the untraceable allusion is the unconscious allusion. A poet writes a line that turns out to be an echo, or even a facsimile, of something he or she has long ago read or heard and then has apparently stored away and forgotten, like a squirrel with too many caches of nuts. A line I wrote about my wedding in 1978 called the grass "green as glass," a phrase I was abashed to find

I had apparently borrowed from a Golden Book, *The Color Kittens*, which my mother read to me before I could read to myself—that is, before about 1954. In another poem, written later, the image "the bath of silence," which at first I thought I'd come up with all by myself, turned out to owe something, even if not its precise phrasing, to the description in George MacDonald's *The Princess and the Goblin*, one of the first books I could and repeatedly did read to myself. The Princess's great-great-grandmother lays the little girl down in an apparently bottomless blue bath, an otherworldly image both alluring and alarming. Recently, though, I came upon a claim that the phrase "bath of silence" originates with Meister Eckhart; both unconscious and untraceable, perhaps.

Not precisely untraceable, but not common or garden either, is the stealth allusion. In Robert Louis Stevenson's *An Inland Voyage*, a delightful book I stumbled on in a Vermont bookstore, the author and his traveling companion eat a mediocre dinner in Quartes: "We had some beefsteak, not so tender as it might have been, some of the potatoes, some cheese, an extra glass of the swipes ["poor weak beer", according to the *OED*] and white sugar in our coffee . . . ." However disappointing the dinner was, the working men dining at the same inn had, the author notes, far worse food, and less of it. Stevenson muses: "According to the Lucretian maxim, our steak should have been flavoured by the look of the other's breadberry. But we did not find it so in practice."

The "maxim" to which Stevenson here alludes is the "suave mari magno" passage that opens Book II of *De*

Rerum Natura. In A. E. Stallings's 2007 translation, "How sweet it is to watch from dry land when the stormwinds roil / A mighty ocean's waters, and see another's bitter toil— / Not because you relish someone else's misery — / Rather, it's sweet to know from what misfortunes you are free."

Not only am I an admirer of Lucretius, but my husband's 1984 piano piece entitled "Suave Mari Magno," which was played at his memorial service (probably the same week I bought the volume of Stevenson), had been much on my mind. It would be interesting to know, though, how many of Stevenson's readers could rely on a "shared body of knowledge," in Rachel Wetzsteon's phrase. Did *suave mari magno* immediately pop into most readers' minds? More of Stevenson's readers probably thought, "Aha, of course," than would have in 2012. But maybe the allusion was fugitive even then.

With all these new subcategories of allusion dancing in my head, I turned back to the *Princeton Encyclopedia.* Considering the many possible tones of allusion, Rachel writes, "It can be lighthearted, as when, in Tom Stoppard's play *Jumpers,* the protagonist George Moore, brooding on violent acts while holding his tortoise Pat, declares, "Now might I do it, Pat." Here Rachel lays out the way Stoppard humorously alludes to *Hamlet,* but her choice of line is so unexpected and characteristic of Rachel that it quickly brings a third into the equation: in addition to Stoppard and Shakespeare we have her, too. One might perhaps call this allusion a signature or clue or fragrance: some evocative and poignant trace.

This charming example strongly brings back my friend and neighbor. Rachel was a gifted and well-read poet who played happily in the fields of allusion—a word whose etymology of course recalls the ludic—but who was eventually engulfed by the difficulties that led her to take her own life late in 2009, at the age of forty-two. "Now might I do it, Pat," a quintessentially Wetzsteonian example of allusion, made me smile. But I paused more soberly over another reference late in the article, where Rachel observes that Christopher Ricks, in his study *Allusion in the Poets*, has "poignantly remarked that allusion can mitigate a writer's loneliness." So it can; allusion can call up quite a crowd of influential ghosts who are for the most part friendly and helpful. In the case of this article's author, who was on such good terms with the trope of allusion, who understood it so well and articulated it with such wit and sympathy, allusion finally didn't mitigate her loneliness enough. Yet that's not quite true. Here's Rachel, a bright presence in the pages of this weighty tome, recognizably witty and precise, sharing her knowledge—now herself an influential ghost to whom I find myself turning with a question to ask or yet another unclassifiable example to share.

LUCRETIUS

I can't remember when I first encountered Lucretius's great, mysterious poem. Could it have been in high school? Maybe it's inaccurate hindsight that tells me I was already a little conversant with *De Rerum Natura* when I took a college course devoted to the poem. Taught by the genial, urbane, and learned J.P. Elder, the course was one of the two best Classics courses I had at Harvard. (Latin love elegy, taught by G.P. Goold, was the other; I was less fortunate in my Greek teachers.) Under the influence of Elder's course, and still, I guess, ignorant of Tennyson's poem about Lucretius, I wrote a dramatic monologue, "Lucretius's Widow Thinks Aloud" which I'm startled to remember as clearly as I do. The poem was published in *The Harvard Advocate* or *The Lion Rampant* or *The Quince*, but never collected. My poem begins:

> You only wanted to get rid of fear.
> Put fear behind you and the sky was open,
> You said; and fear was finally fear of death,
> Shattered and put together cleverly
> With only love left out. Love falsifies
> And men are sickly-spirited enough
> Without confusion.

Almost two decades passed, and I must have gone on being at least conscious of Lucretius. I suggested the title of my husband's 1984 piano solo piece, *Suave Mari Magno*, the phrase which begins the magnificent opening of Book II: "How sweet it is to watch from dry land when the storm-winds roil..." In 1985 Willard Spiegelman gave me his excellent monograph "Some Lucretian Elements in Wordsworth." In 1999 I was lucky enough to make the acquaintance of A.E. Stallings, whose superb translation of Lucretius, published in 2007, I am using in the above quotation. Stallings's amazing achievement is to have rendered *De Rerum Natura* into rhymed fourteeners with accuracy, grace, wit, and inevitability. But it is also true that Lucretius retains some of his unique flavor in any translation. It isn't that, like Cavafy, Lucretius sounds good in anyone's rendering. But he does always sound like himself: urgent, passionate, willful, possessed by the big picture but willing to stop and note details—or unable not to stop. Palmer Bovie and Rolfe Humphries, less felicitous than Stallings, still both capture a good deal of the sheer energy of the poem.

Stephen Greenblatt's 2011 study *The Swerve* has presumably introduced Lucretius to a new generation of readers; New York University held a Lucretius conference in the same year. Lucretius seems to be one of those writers destined to be rediscovered and cherished periodically by people whose interests do not normally encompass Latin or Epicureanism or poetry. A very imperfect analogue to Lucretius's durable but also rarefied reputation might be found not in Wordsworth (though as Spiegelman points out, analogies do abound between Lucretius and Wordsworth) but in Wallace Stevens, who stands apart from many poets of his (or any other) time and whose work means a great deal to many people who don't necessarily count themselves lovers of poetry. Perhaps it's relevant in this connection that we know almost nothing about Lucretius's personal life, and that what we know about Stevens's doesn't help us much with the poetry.

You can dip a finger in Lucretius anywhere and come upon him energetically lecturing, almost hectoring, urging us to pay attention (*nunc age quod superest cognosce et clarius audi*). You can also easily find lush and beautiful passages—the invocation to Venus and the start of Book II are among the more famous, but there are many others, which sometimes form part of his argument, sometimes introduce a point or sum up a section (*tantum religio potuit suadere malorum*) and sometimes feel like a spontaneous effusion of fervor, as if the poet is bursting the boundaries of his own rhetorical structure (*Avia Pieridum peragro loca nullius ante/trita solo...*). There is the unforgettable if also finally unconvincing argument against the fear of death. But there's also a profusion of less famous passages about what Lucretius's title promises: the way the world works. After Hurricane Irene, for example, I felt the need to turn to the passage on floods and lazily asked Alicia Stallings to point me to the right spot, which she obligingly did—for this is not a famous passage. Here it all was—the downed trees, the washed-out bridges. Lucretius might have been describing central Vermont.

De Rerum Natura does not offer narrative or mythology—or rather the only mythology Lucretius serves up is the allegorized anti-mythology of his underworld, where each hellish torture is psychological. The length of the poem in combination with the lack of narrative presents readers with a serious problem, or rather, it would were it not for the onrushing force, not so much of the argument as of the vision. Still, the lack of narrative arc means that the poem isn't a page- turner; we can get swept up in the rhetoric, but we can equally lose ourselves in the beauty or sheer fascination of any number of individual passages. (What causes wet dreams? Why are some people so passive and others so quick to anger? Which is more important, nature or nurture?) No characters, no plot, and yet we go on reading. What holds us is the voice—and any authorial voice, however vigorous, is necessarily at times more compelling than at other times. Hence our attention may wander; hence Lucretius, knowing this to be the case, buttonholes us from time to time. The honey of his verse is surely designed not only to sweeten the bitter cup of atomic theory but to keep us lazy listeners and readers in a good mood.

A long, plotless poem that so tests our attention and patience, while also leaving room for a little mental meandering—this certainly sounds like Wordsworth to me, as it has to Spiegelman and many others. But I am also reminded of the requirements Wallace Stevens sets forth (in his own demanding and plotless longish poem "Notes Toward a Supreme Fiction") for a successful work of the imagination. Stevens's criteria are three: It Must Be Abstract; It Must Change; and It Must Give Pleasure. Lucretius triumphantly meets all three requirements, and in so doing he gives hope and inspiration to all the poets who follow him who aspire to something larger than the single lyric but are not drawn by narrative. In its very strangeness and, yes, abstractness, *De Rerum Natura* has been and continues to be an idiosyncratic blueprint or roadmap for other poets wandering "in the uncharted country of the Muses," those *avia Pieridum* where it was Lucretius's proud and lonely boast that he was a pathfinder.

ON JUDGING A POETRY CONTEST

Poets optimistically assume, or I assume they assume, that their quirks of character enhance their poetry, heightening idiosyncrasy into art. Who am I to dispute this happy assumption? Sometimes it works. This woman's chatty, loose, mildly amusing, long drawn-out lines about her Italian travels emit an aura of improvisation, at once charming and willed, spontaneous and not, that exactly matches my ten-year-old memories of listening to her talk. This man's meditations on Midwestern winters err, on the other hand, on the side of glumness. He makes a good deal of use of the journals of pioneers (his ancestors?) braving hard winters as they cross the plains; but his own lines also have a distinctly wintry feel.

Both these manuscripts, entries in the same contest, are anonymous, so what I'm recognizing are the poets' voices. The term isn't exact—one could also say styles, mannerisms, personalities. James Merrill says somewhere that a poet's voice is a more democratic term for what used to be called "tone." Both manuscripts have made the first cut: her flow and his stiff upper lip have landed in the stack of entries I've set apart as definitely worth another look. The sheaves pile up as I sort them into three stacks:

Probable; Maybe; No. I could call the Probables more accomplished, but it would be truer to say that they're more familiar. I feel as if they are faces or voices that I more or less recognize, even if the writers' names elude me. Evidently my response is less aesthetic than tribal.

Why are certain manuscripts more familiar, recognizable, intelligible? It's a matter of temperament as expressed on the page—of a verbal body-language, so to speak, that appeals to me. Some decorum is being observed, as of an interesting stranger who's fun to talk to at a party but who also doesn't lean in too close. Ms. Long Loose Lines and Mr. Clenched Jaw are temperamentally different, but both observe certain boundaries. Their poems are accessible without being simple-minded; complicated without being hermetic.

I wonder whether my intuitive response to poetry that feels familiar is somehow more valid than my reactions would be if I were judging poems in a vacuum. If the unknown poet's work were speaking to me from a sealed chamber of clinical isolation, would I be a fairer judge? Well, from some manuscripts there does indeed emanate a feeling of antiseptic dissociation. Yet sometimes it is those very poems, poems whose background I can't imagine, whose voices I can hardly hear, that are among the most memorable, even if I don't have a clue as to the gender or age or biography of the author.

The familiar and the unfamiliar poems I'm sorting and stacking on my living room floor, as the cats nose at the growing piles, have this in common: behind the words on the page lie experiences and contingencies which many invisible choices have somehow layered and winnowed into poetry. In the case of the relatively familiar-seeming, user-friendly poems, I can easily (maybe too easily) imagine what these experiences may have been, can hear a voice and almost conjure a face. In the case of the others, the poem speaks to me from a faceless mystery. But all the manuscripts in the Probables pile have managed, in their various ways, to achieve to my satisfaction some version of the transformation "from need to accomplishment." David Kalstone, who uses that phrase in his study *Five Temperaments* (1977), goes on to quote Randall Jarrell's *Poetry and the Age* (1959). "If there were only," Jarrell writes ruefully, "some mechanism ... for reasonably and systematically converting into poetry what we see and feel and are."

There was no such mechanism in 1959 or 1977; there is none in 2012. Jarrell also writes of the "worthless" books that come in day after day that "it is as if the writers had sent you their ripped-out arms and legs, with 'This is a poem' scrawled on them in lipstick." But the manuscripts that go into my No pile remind me more of another remark of Jarrell's, when he said that Oscar Williams's poems read as if they had been written on a typewriter by a typewriter. Update this to "computer" and there you have it. Such poems often look clean and elegant on the page; their writers may have read a great deal, may spell (or spellcheck) well. The poems look plausible. My test: let them sit overnight and see if I remember anything in the morning—an image, a detail, a verb, anything. If it all comes at me freshly, stalely, too familiar and unfamiliar at once, so much untransformed life in my face, on to the No pile it goes.

There is no prescription for good poetry. I tend to advise students to cut, but some poems need more, not less. Revision? Sometimes that just amounts to rearranging the deckchairs. Form? I think it was Charles Martin who said that most twentieth-century villanelles (or was it sestinas) with the exception of Elizabeth Bishop's "One Art" or her "Sestina" might as well be "carted off for landfill." Originality? The disconcerting and reassuring fact is that the best and worst poetry is all occasioned by the same handful of human responses to the world. If we insist on trying to pry loose what the poet is trying to say, or what was known as "theme" when I was in high school, we're likely to come up with such sentiments as "I love you," "it's winter / spring / fall / summer," "someone has died," "I'm happy," "I'm sad"—feelings which do not in themselves guarantee that the poem will fly or sink. In poetry, the how trumps the what.

Many of the poems that end up in teetering piles on my living room floor aren't as raw and dissociative as the ripped-out arms and legs Jarrell thought of when he thought of the unwashed mass of poetry. Rather, they are conscientious, understandable and often admirably thorough efforts to make sense of flux and change and loss: to hold on to something in the face of oblivion. Even if they don't make the cut—my cut, whatever that means— perhaps such poems have accomplished something, if only momentarily, for their writers and also perhaps for their intended audiences, whoever those readers or hearers may have been. Philip Larkin said that it was a positive thing to write even a negative poem.

As I readjust the piles of submissions, isn't some such encounter what I (and the writers whose work I am considering) am hoping for? The winning manuscript may be one that only made it into my Yes pile by a whisker. But once that manuscript goes out into the world, if it does, then a poem in it, or even a single line of a poem, may prove to be exactly what some reader needed.

I leave the piles for the night. I'll check them again in the morning, to see if anything has changed.

Sam & Lycidas

I. In the attic

Early last June, I spent a week in northern Vermont. My old house was in a state of radical de- and re-construction, so I stayed down the road at the house (also an old house) of neighbors of many years' standing who were more like family than friends.

My little sleeping alcove, decorously arranged with a curtain suspended from a clothesline, was located in a cozy corner of the Holden house's vast attic. I was fascinated by the richness and variety of the attic's contents. The books it contained were enough to keep any bibliophile busy for a month of rainy days. I'll get back to those books later. But books were far from being all that the attic contained.

The detritus of at least three generations of a large family, objects accumulated or cast off (but not thrown away) over a period of forty years or more, were in evidence, if not in order, up here. Harold Holden, the father of the family, had died the previous spring. The five adult children and their children and in some cases grandchildren had—as who does not?—far-flung and complicated lives. "Children grow up and go away," Harold's widow Janet said to me sometime during my stay, "and they leave their lives behind." Or else they come back to the nest for a while, or for more than a while, and bring pieces of their changing lives with them. One daughter had moved with her husband first to Oregon, and then to Mexico. They had left behind so many cartons of books that these spilled over from the attic into the barn. The youngest daughter had recently sold her house in Burlington and moved, with her share of that house's contents and the younger of her two teenage sons—where but back to this old house? And so it went.

As is the way of storage spaces, the attic had become at once an archaeological site and an allegory. Relics of the late patriarch rubbed shoulders with children's and grandchildren's toys, artwork, schoolbooks, hobby projects, and other possessions. A hatbox, watercolor sets, a pair of slippers, an umbrella stand, an armchair piled high with pillowcases and blankets, a chess set, a half-finished painting on the table by the window, a broken kite, a toy soldier... As I looked around the attic and tried to take stock, the impulse to make a list was almost irresistible.

That table by the attic's sole window looked like an inviting place to sit and write. I glanced around, but all the unbroken chairs were apparently being used as surfaces on which to pile things; so I returned to my inventory, as if simply cataloguing the contents of this confusing space were a first step toward carving order out of the clutter. Perhaps making a catalogue is such a step. More likely, naming things is a way of trying to remember why it's important to keep them. Hugo Williams writes evocatively in a recent "Freelance" article of his various "systems... for clearing things out," a process that proves nearly impossible.

Some objects, for example,

> seem to accumulate on every surface, each with its own special plea for exemption. These are evaluated according to whether I still know what they are, or care. Out go the rocks, the shells, the scent bottles and tobacco tins, a bell pull, a hubcap, a tax disc, a Perspex antery, Real Indian War Paints ("Wet your Finger and Paint your Face") and an ancient packet of "Optios" powder mix: "Hot Chocolate with a Smooth Milky Taste" . . . . Once things are out of the house it's like lancing a boil, the pain gradually decreases and the hole heals over with new dust.

Times Literary Supplement 8/20-27/2010

Obedient to the itemizing impulse, even though these were not my attic, my family, my possessions, or my memories, I drifted between the dusty piles, holding a pen and a notebook, even though there was no place to sit down, and added to the list: a broken suitcase or two, a chest; half a rocking chair; a cat carrier; a three-legged nightstand.

The poetry, the possibilities of attics! What precisely is their attraction? In part, we respond to architecture: the richness of what Mervyn Peake in *Gormenghast* calls "the language of dim stairs and moth-hung rafters."

(How eloquently these nine words, which form a perfect pentameter line, inflect space with both poetry and humanity.) Gaston Bachelard in *The Poetics of Space* authoritatively unpacks the way a small attic can contain an entire world of private memory:

> all the spaces of our past moments of solitude, the spaces in which we have suffered from solitude, remain indelible within us, and precisely because the human being wants them to remain so. He knows instinctively that this space identified with his solitude is creative.... In the past, the attic may have seemed too small, it may have seemed cold in winter and hot in summer. Now, however, in memory recaptured through daydreams, it is hard to say through what a syncretism the attic is at once small and large, warm and cool, always comforting . . . .We always go up the attic stairs, which are steeper and more primitive. For they bear the mark of ascension to a more tranquil solitude. When I return to dream in the attic of yesteryear, I never go down again.

Those steep stairs that go only one way: I recognize them from the first book I ever read (and then reread again and again) to myself, George MacDonald's The *Princess and the Goblin.* MacDonald deals quite honestly with the fact that little Princess Irene, an only child whose mother is dead, whose King-Papa is nearly always away, and whose nurse is very limited, is often bored. The attic is a refuge from boredom, a source of adventure. But it is also, as MacDonald understands, the source and heart of boredom. Bachelard: "There are children who will leave a game to go and be bored in the corner of a garret. How often have I wished for the attic of my boredom when the complications of life made me lose the very germ of all freedom!" I remember a Peanuts cartoon from my childhood that my family thought applied pretty well to my behavior. Charlie Brown: "Lucy, would you like to go out and play?" Lucy: "No, I think I'll stay in and fuss."

The dreamy freedom so nostalgically evoked by Bachelard bears a family resemblance to boredom in that it lacks the obligations, complications, and general scurrying busyness of the adult world.

In C. S. Lewis's *The Magician's Nephew*, Diggory explains to Polly the appeal of the attic-like crawl space under the row-house roof where they retire to play. This space isn't exactly an attic, but it's certainly not a house either. He says:

> Think of our tunnel under the slates at home. It isn't a room in any of the houses. In a way, it isn't really a part of any of the houses. But once you're in the tunnel you can go along it and come out into any of the houses in the row.

Diggory draws an analogy between this non-space of a tunnel and the magical wood where he and Polly find themselves:

> Mightn't this wood be the same?—a place that isn't in any of the worlds, but once you've found that place you can get into them all— And of course that explains everything... That's why it is so quiet and sleepy here. Nothing ever happens here. Like at home. It's in the house that people talk, and do things, and have meals. Nothing goes on in the in-between places, behind the

walls and above the ceilings and under the floor or in our own tunnel. But when you come out of our tunnel you may find yourself in any house. I think we can get out of this place into jolly well Anywhere!

One escapes to the attic to be bored, to dream, and to go on magical journeys such as Diggory and Polly find themselves in the midst of. Attics also afford a vantage point from which to observe literally or figuratively the everyday life going on downstairs. In *The Princess and the Goblin*, as in *Gormenghast*, the hot noisy kitchen in the bowels of the house serves as the downstairs to the dreamy, lonely upstairs of the child at play. MacDonald (1824-1905) and Bachelard (1884-1962) both grew up in the world of Upstairs-Downstairs, a world from which Mervyn Peake (1911-1968) wasn't so far distant in time either.

The Holdens' attic, whose contents I've been making an abortive attempt to itemize, is actually the first of two adjacent attics—a sort of anteroom to an even more distilled attic experience. (Interestingly, Fuchsia's private attic in *Gormenghast* turns out to have two or even three chambers opening out of one another.) To enter the second attic here, one opens a door and picks one's way through various more or less bulky, shrouded shapes in a gloomy chamber lit by—again—a single window.

This second attic sounds like a déjà vu, a figment, an example of mythological reduplication. But it's real, and it has its own distinctive character. For one thing, attic number two lacks electric light. You have to grope your way past a spinning wheel, a churn, boxes of china, and an old sofa, to name a few, to get close to that lone window at the far end. There are no chairs here, any more than there are in the first attic. But it's possible to sit down near the window on a bare mattress, sneezing from the bits of straw and dust mites that glitter in the air when a sunbeam cuts across the space. A better place to sit, though, is right on the floor. Between the wide, rickety old floorboards of attic number two, cracks abound. Choose your spot, look down, and you can easily spy, through the chinks between the boards, life going on downstairs—that place where, as Diggory says, people talk and have meals and do things. Someone is standing at the kitchen counter stirring something. Someone else is washing dishes. A conversation— messages, reminders, a mild disagreement?—is in progress. The phone rings and someone answers it.

All attics partake of the symbolic. But this inner attic in the Holden house seemed to me especially uncanny. Sitting crosslegged up there for a while one day during my week upstairs, partly privy, in an involuntarily way, to the daily doings down below, I felt a little like Princess Irene, a little like Fuchsia, a little like Diggory, and a little like the revenant Emily when she comes back from the dead in *Our Town* and finds herself in the kitchen while her mother prepares breakfast. Irene, Diggory, and Fuchsia are all fictional young people. Emily is not only imaginary but, in the scene I'm thinking of, she's dead. I, on the other hand, am sixty-one years old and alive. But from the vantage point of the attic, these distinctions seem remarkably unimportant.

Attics are not only treasure troves of allegory; they're nurseries of dreams. When we're not actually in attics, we may well dream about them, or about attic-like spaces. Bachelard: "even when we no longer have a garret, when the attic room is lost and gone, there remains the fact that we once loved a garret, once lived in an attic. We return to them in our night dreams..." And when we're lucky enough to be sleeping in an attic, we dream of other places.

The nights I spent in my curtained alcove I was one of four sleepers in the Holdens' attic. The four of us comprised two mother-son dyads. We each had our own sleeping space; the other three sleepers (my twenty-six-year-old son; the returned daughter; her thirteen-year-old son) each had their own room. All four of us were in transition, moving through changes in where and how we lived. Did we all negotiate the same journey in our sleep? Did we use the night hours either to look back over a shoulder and wave a farewell or else, turning from the past to future, to greet whoever or whatever was approaching?

To me, at least, the big dusty dim attic did seem to be conducive to sound sleep. Between worn sheets laundered to a delicious softness, I lay next to my husband. No, that's wrong; he was long gone, and also not gone; still alive, alive perhaps for many years to come, in the city. What I was lying next to was his almost palpable absence. In the morning, all four of us woke from whatever our respective dreams had been to milky brightness at the single window—a window to which my little alcove was closest. Spring rain was pattering on the roof. Real life, so called, beckoned; we went down the stairs (down the attic stairs!) to eat breakfast and to do whatever the day demanded.

It's clear that I've abandoned my abortive inventory of objects in these attics. Such an inventory was never going to be finished or finishable anyway. But I returned, later that day, later that week, again and again, to what so far I have barely mentioned but what for me were always the heart of the Holdens' attic, and for that matter the heart of their house: the books.

II. Books

For Hugo Williams too, the process of clearing out is the most intractable when it comes to books:

> Books are the hardest things to get rid of because of their closedness and changeability. It isn't enough to hate a book for you to get rid of it: you might need it some time for that very reason. You find yourself trying to distinguish between awful and boring, until some boring book looks strangely fascinating and you waste a morning on it.

Mornings get wasted this way because of the unique power of books to suck us into another world. It's not just that a reader can look up to find that hours have passed. The story also inflects your experience of the world outside books. Tony Hiss describes the effect of a child steeping himself in books in *The View from Alger's Window*, a book that is ostensibly about his father Alger Hiss but is really more concerned with the imagination of both father and son. Being deeply absorbed in a book, Hiss writes,

> doesn't mean drowning out the world by reading stories. It means throwing yourself so far into a story that that's where you actually live, curled up in one corner of a house belonging to one of the characters... you could still stay in the story even when you weren't reading. There were rules, of course,—you had to leave once you finished a book, but if you stopped in the middle because you had to do something else, such as setting the table, then that's where you actually remained, on that same page, for the whole time that you appeared to be setting the table. It's sort of the reverse of an out-of-body experience, because it felt as though you had sent your body out into the world while you stayed invisibly inside, next to the bookmark.

This absorbing sense of inwardness and otherness—of what Eve Kosofsky Sedgwick calls the inner space of the life of the mind—that books provide was palpable in the Holdens' attic. I could note old sewing machines, dishes, chess sets, hatboxes; but books I could get lost in. Harold, the late father of the family, had been a man of many talents and avocations. In addition to being a photographer, inventor, musician, poet, and carpenter, he had been a student and teacher of literature. The books in the attic that had clearly belonged to him represented a long lifetime of devoted and eclectic reading. I won't attempt to indicate the range of Harold's taste with yet another list. But I could scarcely put my hand out without finding a book which looked, as Hugo Williams puts it, "strangely fascinating," without even necessarily being boring.

Whether I find myself in a thrift shop vaguely seeking a sweater or among bookshelves, my guiding principle is a kind of restless serendipity—I put my hand out and see what I've come up with. As it happened, though, the week I spent in the Holdens' attic I was actually looking for a book. More specifically, I wanted the text of a poem: Milton's *Lycidas*. I certainly had access to more than one copy of this poem at home, but I wanted to reread the poem freshly here and now. Sure enough, here among Harold's books was a red Modern Library Milton. I turned straight to *Lycidas*.

III. Lycidas

I was particularly in search of the poem's opening; specifically, its first seventeen lines. For Sam Levin, the person to whom I owed my renewed attentiveness to *Lycidas*, and who loves to recite the poem taking it from the top, never gets any farther than "sweep the string."

Here were the lines I had been hearing so often, in one iteration or another, for the past year but hadn't actually reread for way too long.

Yet once more, O ye Laurels, and once more
Ye Myrtles brown, with Ivy never sere,
I come to pluck your Berries harsh and crude,
And with forc'd fingers rude
Shatter your leaves before the mellowing year.
Bitter constraint, and sad occasion dear,
Compels me to disturb your season due:
For Lycidas is dead, dead ere his prime
Young Lycidas, and hath not left his peer:
Who would not sing for Lycidas? He knew
Himself to sing, and build the lofty rhyme.
He must not flote upon his watry bier
Unwept, and welter to the parching wind,
Without the meed of some melodious tear.

Begin then, Sisters of the sacred well,
That from beneath the seat of Jove doth spring,
Begin, and somewhat loudly sweep the string.

The Sam-Lycidas connection works like this: Sam, ninety-three, lives at the 80th Street Residence, the dementia facility that has been my husband's home for two years now. Until fairly recently, Sam and George, my husband, lived on the same floor, so I got to know Sam and his daughter Amy, a woman my age, fairly well. And when I visited, I and anyone else who was around often got to hear Sam's spirited if truncated rendition of *Lycidas*.

When Sam first moved to 80th Street in the spring of 2009, Amy told me that he had been a professor of linguistics at CUNY. I took a couple of his books out of the Rutgers library, but I couldn't understand them very well. These books were about, among other more obscure topics, metaphors, a subject that interests me. Sam clearly loved poetry (he refers to Wordsworth often), but the context and arguments tended to elude me—no doubt I wasn't trying very hard. There was little actual poetry that I recall quoted in his books; certainly *Lycidas* doesn't make an appearance. "He never seemed especially fond of *Lycidas*," said Amy once. "I didn't know he knew any of it by heart." Yet somewhere in Sam's memory these seventeen lines were securely lodged, ready to burst forth afresh: not ideas about the thing but the thing itself.

"Yet once more, oh ye laurels," Sam would begin. How fitting that three of the six words in the poem's opening phrase refer to iteration. With each successive performance, Sam would indeed be reciting yet once more, just as Amy and I would be listening yet once more to his rendition, as would be Sam's neighbors on the ninth floor, George and Mary and Kit and Irene, or the regular ninth floor aides Monica and Latoya. Amy's husband John might be there too, and Mary's daughters and grandchildren. All of us could and often nearly did sing along as (yet once more) Sam got as far as "Begin, and somewhat loudly sweep the string." He delivered this last line with such panache and authority that it sounded both like an end and like a beginning, which is precisely what this line is, as Milton simultaneously winds up his invocation and moves us toward the poem's body.

Crouched in the attic with the red book in my hand, I was struck by the seamless way in which lines fifteen through seventeen,

> Begin then, Sisters of the sacred well,
> That from beneath the seat of Jove doth spring,
> Begin, and somewhat loudly sweep the string.

at once unfold from and sum up (with the help of the word "then") the lines that have preceded them. And yet lines ten and eleven ("Who would not sing for *Lycidas*? He knew/Himself to sing, and build the lofty rhyme") and line fourteen ("Without the meed of some melodious tear") are both not only end-stopped but sound definitively strong; syntax, music, and meaning all ordain a pause.

I was the more aware of such pauses because Sam sometimes stops his recitation at line eleven or fourteen; he sometimes but not always gets as far as seventeen. But whether he stops at line eleven, line fourteen, or line seventeen, these are all natural endings. He never stopped in the middle of a line, a clause, or a thought.

I had realized, listening to Sam over the past year, that I too was uncertain as to the precise syntax (and secondarily, punctuation which varies from one edition of the poem to another) of the poem *Lycidas*, which was why I'd needed to consult the text. I also wanted to go on to revisit, in a more general sort of way, the 176 lines of *Lycidas* Sam never reached when he recited the poem. All these lines proved to be familiar, though I certainly couldn't have recited the poem from beginning to end.

IV. Lycidas the Classic

I doubt if it was Sam's plan to provide a canonical nudge. But his recitations reawakened my interest in the idea of the poem *Lycidas* as well as redirecting my attention to specific lines in the text. When I located the *Lycidas* in the crowded attic, I found myself thinking afresh about what a classic is.

Italo Calvino in his pregnant essay "Why Read the Classics?" provides several overlapping definitions of the term, all of which I like even when (or especially because) they contradict one another. Here are four of them: "A classic is a work which relegates the noise of the present to a background hum, which at the same time the classics cannot exist without." "A classic is a work which persists as background noise when even the present that is wholly incompatible with it holds sway." "A classic is a work which constantly generates a pulviscular cloud of critical discourse around it, but which always shakes the particles off." "A classic is a book which even when we read it for the first time gives the sense of rereading something we have read before." To which I'd add another definition: a classic is a work that you instinctively know you'll find in any well-stocked attic; and that indeed you need only to put out your hand to touch.

In the vicinity of the Modern Library Milton on the attic bookshelf were several hefty literature textbooks. Such tomes, especially when their focus is poetry, have in recent years become something of a hobby of mine. I don't collect them with any thoroughness, but I buy them now and then and am usually glad I did, for they often contain unsuspected riches.

The book I now pulled off the shelf—it was adjacent to the Milton— was *Criticism: The Foundations of Literary Judgment, Revised Edition* (1948; 1958). I'm not sure what I was looking for; but it didn't take me long to find in *Foundations*, which had been edited by Mark Schorer, Josephine Miles, and Gordon McKenzie, part of what Calvino refers to as the cloud of critical discourse that a classic generates. For this solid, charcoal-gray textbook turned out to contain not one but two critical excerpts devoted to *Lycidas*—proof enough, if I were seeking proof, of the poem's classic status.

Curious to see what these two critics had to say about the poem, I investigated rather lazily, skimming along in a way that in my experience great poetry discourages but that critical prose seems to encourage. Paul Elmer More's 1936 essay "How to Read *Lycidas*" didn't detain me long— for one thing, in its decorous meanderings the essay didn't immediately seem, to my impatient browsing at least, to live up to the promise of its title, which in a less formal age might have been "My Problem with Milton" or "Annoying Personality, Great Poem." More lived from 1864-1937, so the essay, written at the end of his life, revisits Milton and in the process unfolds its author's mixed feelings about him.

Unfair though it is to cherry-pick a quote from More's densely argued essay, I plan to do just that. More has just been caviling at Tennyson's praise of Milton as a "Mighty-mouth'd inventor of harmonies... God-gifted organ voice of England," and proceeds to discriminate. He (More) isn't as awed by Milton's genius as Tennyson was, but neither can he agree with what he discreetly dubs "a school of modern critics and poets" in condemning Milton's style. Here is the passage:

> Now, if there be any hesitation with me to accept Milton's style as the norm of good English, it is certainly not on the ground of that "dissociation of sensibility" which draws a school of modern critics and poets to repudiate what may be called the Miltonic line of development and to seek their parentage in Shakespeare and Donne and the "Metaphysicals." If I understand what the leader of that Choir means by this rather obscure phrase, it is that Milton by conscious choice and judgment dissociated his mind from one whole range of perceptions . . . .

When More refers with feline fastidiousness to "a school of modern critics and poets," he is of course thinking of T. S. Eliot, the unnamed "leader of that Choir," and specifically of Eliot's influential 1921 essay "The Metaphysical Poets," in which Eliot famously set forth his theory of "a dissociation of sensibility... from which we have never recovered." This dissociation, Eliot claimed, "was aggravated by the influence of the two most powerful poets of the century, Milton and Dryden." When More observes that the modern school "seek their parentage" in the poetry of Shakespeare and Donne and the "Metaphysicals" rather than in that of Milton, he strikes precisely the genealogical note Eliot was so fond of when he engaged in his confident cobbling together of family traits along the lines of poetic tradition.

The above passage from More is really something of a sidebar in his essay about Milton. At most, it is a parenthetical transition to what More thinks is wrong with Milton, which isn't what Eliot and company think. But (still in the attic) I found myself more interested in this passing reference to Eliot than in More's continuing discussion of Milton. For one thing, More's essay takes a very long time getting down to cases about the actual poem *Lycidas*, whereas More allows himself plenty of room to ponder Milton's prose, personality, reputation, and so on.

The very fact that More is so interested in Eliot's dismissal of Milton that he glides from considering Milton to considering Eliot is surely symptomatic of what Calvino calls "the... cloud of discourse generated by a classic." That is, the canonical poem *Lycidas* is the occasion for More to ponder Eliot's theory of the dissociation of sensibility. (Not that Eliot mentions *Lycidas* in "The Metaphysical Poets"; but he does mention Milton). The passage I quoted above could easily be scooped out of its context and declared aim as a reading of Milton's poem and inserted into a textbook on critical theory as an example of a critic using a text as a stick with which (however politely) to tap, if not to beat, another critic.

Come to think of it, wasn't what I was holding in my dusty hands a textbook of critical theory? Yes, certainly. It had probably been a teaching text of Harold's. But a striking difference between *Criticism: The Foundations of Modern Literary Judgment* and literary theory textbooks from the early twenty-first century is that the latter so sternly relegate the actual texts critics write about to the wings, while the critic stands in the limelight. In *Criticism*, by contrast, there is no obvious pecking order—the critical approaches are important, but then so are the texts they treat.

I still wondered, though: to what degree were the students (and were these graduate students? Advanced or even not so advanced undergrads?) who were assigned to read *Criticism* in their literature classes expected to follow the fraught if generally polite disagreements about how to approach canonical texts like *Lycidas*—disagreements that Eliot had done much to foment? Paging back to the front matter of the textbook, I noted the editors do confess that "we have been in the habit of approaching criticism not directly, but by bringing it to bear on specially selected texts." Later generations of textbooks tend to approach criticism so directly that they are able to do an end run around the texts themselves.

More's essay, as I've said, failed to keep the promise of its title: to tell the reader how to read *Lycidas*. Telling myself I'd go back to it another day, I found the second piece on *Lycidas* that *Criticism* had to offer—a piece that proved much more compelling.

Let me pause for a moment, though, to consider that idea of going back. So much of reading in the second half of life does mean going back. And not only going back through reading, but going back through what life offers us as well, which includes books but is hardly restricted to them. Sam's recitation had sent me back to *Lycidas*, which, in the Holden attic's welter of books, had sent me via *Criticism* to Paul Elmer More, who, writing in 1936, was at least as preoccupied by T. S. Eliot's 1921 essay on the Metaphysical Poets as he was by Milton's 1637 poem. More's essay, which I read in 2010, seemed more like a period piece than *Lycidas* did—an example of what the inexhaustible Calvino may have in mind when he says that a classic "relegates the noise of the present to a background hum."

It was odd to think that Sam's spirited if truncated rendering of *Lycidas* had sent me by a meandering path to this book of all the books on the attic shelf, and that in precisely this fat volume I had now come upon two essays on *Lycidas*, one of which (and I'll get to it in a minute) was definitively worth this detour, even if its relation to Milton's poem was somewhat tangential. The process of reading, leapfrogging from one text to the next, is nothing if not tangential. This very fortuitousness is what Robert Frost has in mind when he writes in "The Figure a Poem Makes" that scholars get their knowledge "with conscientious thoroughness along projected lines of logic; poets theirs cavalierly and as it happens in and out of books. They stick to nothing deliberately but let what will stick to them like burrs where they walk in the fields."

The second piece on *Lycidas* that I found in *Criticism* was, as I say, more compelling. Its author was a poet I admire, John Crowe Ransom, and its intriguing title was "A Poem Nearly Anonymous." This essay was an extract from Ransom's 1938 book *The World's Body* (another striking title), a book of whose existence I had been vaguely aware (something else to return to at a later date). Ransom himself was a vivid presence to me. I had taught some of his poems in a graduate seminar earlier that spring, and the students had been as surprised and delighted as I had hoped they would be by Ransom's unique diction and tart humor. "A Poem Nearly Anonymous" had, I noticed (unlike More's essay), seized the attention of a previous reader of Criticism, probably Harold himself; this reader had heavily annotated the essay in bright pink ink. I understood the impulse; Ransom is eminently quotable.

The prose in "A Poem Nearly Anonymous" proved to be as witty and perspicacious as poems like "Dead Boy" and "Crocodile" had led me to expect of Ransom. The passage I especially noted was somewhat like More's stricture on "the school of modern poets and critics" (i.e. Eliot and company) in that Ransom is using Lycidas as a jumping-off point for a discussion of, or maybe a digression about, contemporary poetics and poetry. But where More disapproves of Eliot's reasons for disapproving of Milton, Ransom does something much more useful. He employs Milton's use of pastoral elegy as an occasion for explaining how persona poetry works. Thereby Ransom not only, like the good teacher he undoubtedly was, casts light on a difficult poem, but also segues into a consideration of poems by Ransom's own younger contemporaries.

If, in Frost's phrase, "poets let knowledge stick to them like burrs where they walk in the fields," the burr, or cluster of burrs, that stuck to me as I read Ransom's "A

Poem Nearly Anonymous" was his excellent discussion of the degree to which poems are either anonymous (Ransom explains that he uses the term figuratively), that is, uttered by a masked figure, or else private, personal, and autobiographically true. This distinction proved timely and helpful to my own thinking about poetry—no matter that it had been written in the mid 1930s. After all, *Lycidas*, published in 1637, is perennially durable.

I like to say to my students that poems must float free of their original occasions if they are to have any life beyond their writer's own experience. Ransom puts it much better:

> Anonymity, of some if not literal sort, is a condition of poetry. A good poem, even if it is signed with a full and well-known name, intends as a work of art to lose the identity of the author; that is, it means to represent him not actualized, like an eye-witness testifying in court and held strictly by zealous counsel to the point at issue, but freed from his juridical or prose self and taking an ideal or fictitious personality; otherwise his evidence amounts the less to poetry. Poets may go to universities and... increase greatly the stock of ideal selves into which they may pass for the purpose of being poetical. If on the other hand they insist too narrowly on their own identity and their own story, inspired by a simple but mistaken theory of art, they find their little poetic fountains drying up within them.

Notice with what silky urbanity Ransom moves, in the middle of this passage, from an almost impersonal laying down of a timeless law of the poetic art to an observation based presumably on his own experience as a professor.

Elegant, too, is the way in which, at the end of the passage, he makes use of a pastoral figure for inspiration that was old when Milton, wearing the mask of a shepherd but speaking as a poet, wrote in *Lycidas* (albeit in a passage Sam never reached in his renditions): "For we were nurst upon the self-same hill,/Fed the same flock, by fountain, shade, and rill."

I thought, in this connection, of Frost's "The Pasture," a little poem that serves as a proem to Frost's oeuvre: "I'm going out to clean the pasture spring./I'll only stop to rake the leaves away,/And wait to watch the water clear: I may. /I shan't be gone long.—You come too." Make no mistake: that pasture spring isn't just any pasture spring. It is a version of *Lycidas*'s "fountain, shade, and rill."

Writing before the advent of MFA writing programs, confessional poetry, or identity politics, Ransom seems prescient in his preoccupations. Even if we don't agree with his diagnosis of why some young poets' "little fountains of art" dry up (and which poets precisely does he have in mind? Like More, he is reluctant to name names), Ransom has undeniably put his finger on a trend that surely became more marked in the fifties than it was when he wrote "A Poem Almost Anonymous."

Skilled lecturer that he is, Ransom loops back from his little digression on young poets to Milton, without so much as a paragraph break. With that digression lending emphasis and timeliness to his point, Ransom explains why it made sense for Milton, when he wrote *Lycidas*, to don the mask or mantle of a shepherd in order to eulogize his friend and fellow poet Edward King. The following passage is more helpful than anything in More's essay in guiding the reader through what may now seem the artificiality of *Lycidas*.

> Milton set out to write a poem mourning a friend and poet who had died; in order to do it he became a Greek shepherd, mourning another one. It was not that authority attached particularly to the discourse of a Greek shepherd; the Greek shepherd in his own person would have been hopeless; but Milton as a Greek shepherd was delivered from being Milton the scrivener's son, the Master of Arts from Cambridge, the handsome and finicky young man, and that was the point.

Ransom then swivels briefly back to his complaint about the young (shall we say proto-confessional?) poets of his day, who

> try to become poets on another plan, with rather less success.... they write some of their intense experiences, their loves, pities, griefs, and religious ecstasies; but too literally, faithfully, piously, ingenuously. They seem to want to do without wit and playfulness, dramatic sense, detachment, and it cuts them off from the practice of an art.

Wit and playfulness, dramatic sense, detachment: it's very hard to think of better words than these to describe Ransom's own poetic style, which—at once barbed and heartbreaking, stilted and comical—isn't at all easy to convey with any crispness. Was Ransom then intentionally using *Lycidas* as a background noise to his own poetic concerns? Not exactly; he also has much to say in "A Poem Nearly Anonymous" about Milton's poem in relation to Milton's prose, for example, and also about Milton's Spenserian and Italian influences. But at least at some points in his essay Ransom is writing as a poet as much as he's writing as a critic.

The next time I teach Ransom's work, I'll refer students to this essay on *Lycidas* in part for what it can tell them about Ransom's poetry. For his musings on *Lycidas* triumphantly transcend their immediate occasion—as indeed *Lycidas* does too. Questions of form and function and taste (all of which Ransom also explores in this essay); the poet's assumption of a persona, which we've seen he is eager to explain and defend—these issues do not go away from one generation of poets to the next. They arise, fresh and enigmatic as ever, out of the dustiest out-of-print textbook, just as they do out of Milton's durably mysterious and beautiful elegy. Which is surely how books in attics work. Rummaging around, we may find what we wanted, and next to that something else that's relevant. And then what Hugo Williams calls the "closedness and changeability" of books takes over, and we get lost.

V. Sam and Lycidas

I've said that the place where I met Sam and heard him recite *Lycidas* was the 80th Street Residence —a place

where people are sent, or maybe relegated, when their
lives downstairs, the place where things happen, are
over. Perhaps it is too fanciful to think of the Residence
as a kind of attic too—a place that, as Diggory explains
in *The Magician's Nephew*, "isn't in any of the worlds, but
once you've found that place you can get into them all."
Diggory is comparing the drowsy potential of the Wood
Between the Worlds to the attic-like tunnel where the
children play. Not much playing goes on at 80th Street,
but there's plenty of drowsiness, and, as in an attic, plenty
of accumulation— except that much of the accumulation
is invisible. Instead of old furniture shrouded in dust
sheets, it's a matter of memories waiting to be tapped,
stories told, poems recited. The lives of the people who
arrive at 80th Street can be said to be over, in a sense.
In another sense, so long as the residents can speak,
unexpected vitality can pop out.

My stay in the Holdens' attic took place in early June
2010. I'm writing this in December of the same year. In
November, Sam died. He'd been moved from the sunny
ninth floor at 80th Street down to the darker, lower-
ceilinged second floor, where there were more aides per
number of residents. The recitations were over. Sam had
stopped reciting, stopped eating, pretty much stopped
speaking. He was ready to go, and the journey was a
relatively short one. Another man now inhabits his room.
But the memory of Sam's recitals remains vivid and clear,
full of energy and zest.

One reason Sam liked to recite *Lycidas* was surely that
the poem's opening salvo, "Yet once more," charged with

the anonymity of which Ransom writes (we don't know precisely who "I" in line three is, nor, as Ransom argues, should we know), left space for him to flow effortlessly into the role of bardic reciter. "Yet once more" serves as a platform or pedestal to highlight what is now called performativity—the poem's performativity but also the living man's. "Yet once more," writes Milton; "Yet once more," declaims "the uncouth swain"; "Yet once more," says Sam, his voice suddenly full of authority and gusto. The three words signal his intention to recite. And yet once more, Sam's audience settle themselves comfortably and prepare to listen.

SNAKES

A double spread of gleaming coils: the snake book lies open on the table. Here, I think, is the snake I saw the other day sunning itself perilously in the middle of the dirt road in Danville, Vermont. It's long and stout, elegantly mottled in a pattern of rust, tan and cream, with maybe some faded black. Not your average slender, greenish, striped garter snake, which seldom ventures out of the grass. And here on the facing page is something like the snake Curt saw recently. "I swear," he says, "it was spotted with magenta ovals."

Curt and I are contemporaries; I've known him for half a century. He is also a former neighbor. His late father Harold, a charismatic and versatile man who was a graduate student of my father's at Columbia in the late 1940s, bought a house on this Danville road from my half-brother David in the early 1960s. It's a rambling farmhouse with a big barn. (Harold's widow still inhabits it.) The place's former owner was a farmer named Frank Wynn, and the very steep quarter-mile of dirt road beyond the house, heading precipitously downhill to a brook, was locally known as Wynn's High Dive. When the town decreed that every dirt road should have a name, someone seems to have misheard; the road is now Winn High Drive, which sounds like an ad for a lottery.

Curt and I were children when his father bought the house. But behind my rust-spotted specimen and Curt's magenta ovals, there lurks an ancestral snake, a tutelary house snake that Harold and David reportedly stumbled on behind the Wynn place. I can imagine the scene: a damp summer day, the two men going over the property, floundering around in tall, wet grass out back, wrestling with the cover of an old well. They lift it off to check the water level, or something, and there, coiled under the cover or among the stones, they see a big snake. The rumor of this snake has persisted in my family over the decades. Like a fish, the snake grows in the telling.

In the Geometric period, so one theory goes, Greek potters and epic poets competed, spurring one another on to fresh feats of monumentality, all in a style which combined symmetry and simplicity. Thus the huge amphora in New York's Metropolitan Museum, far too heavy to lift but presumably useful for storage and display, is decorated with tidy bands of stick figures—charioteers, horses, troops, pall-bearers, in a repeating pattern. Symmetry, simplicity, a monumental scale: these features tend towards a schematic abstraction. In his book *Homer and the Heroic Tradition*, published in 1958, Cedric Whitman suggests that the plot of the Iliad has a corresponding symmetry, so that the first and last books correspond, and so on. Whether or not this is a compelling case, the Iliad certainly resembles the amphora at the Met in its outspoken bigness—a cultural artifact intended to overwhelm by its sheer scale.

So in successive tellings, not only did that snake under the well-cover increase in size, but its pattern grew more severely schematic. David and Harold apparently disagreed on the precise look of the reptile they'd seen. Striped? Spotted? They compromised by agreeing to call it plaid—a sort of formalized predecessor of the more free-form blobs of color to which, half a century later, Curt and I were witness.

The week the field guide to snakes lay open on the table was the same week my son and I went to see the ineffably over-the-top movie *Snakes on a Plane* at the local theatre—a film I was reminded of when I caught part (the tail end, I was going to say) of *Anaconda* at the gym sometime later. Snake references aren't lacking at a loftier cultural level, from Dickinson's narrow fellow in the grass to Lawrence's snake or Stevens's bodiless serpent or the immense snake, Loki's daughter, evoked with almost tender fascination in A. S. Byatt's *Ragnarok*. Most of these snakes (Lawrence's is the exception that proves the rule) are hard to see. One vanishes in the grass, one is described as "Skin flashing to wished-for disappearances," one, as well as living under water, is too huge to take in. All are uncanny in the way they silently appear and vanish. We can pore over the field guides, but the real snake is out of sight.

Sidewinder, my husband used to call certain people— possibly an expression he picked up on the Boy Scout ranch in Philmont, New Mexico. He often told me about the time the boys killed a rattler; after chopping off and burying its head, they cooked and ate the body, which (how did I know?) tasted like chicken. These days, when I visit my sister in Albuquerque I like to pay a visit to the Rattlesnake Museum. This ramshackle place houses rattlers from all over the world—one, perhaps from Australia, is an elegant cream and orange mix like a ginger cat. All are stamped with some version of the rattlesnake pattern.

The proprietor of the Rattlesnake Museum was a high school science teacher until he decided to follow his bliss, as Joseph Campbell would say, which led him to establish his museum in a low-ceilinged building piled high with cages, where you can buy T-shirts, keychains, shot glasses, and beer mugs all marked with the rattlesnake logo. "How long does a rattlesnake live in captivity?" I ask, feeling a bit like Hamlet chatting with the gravedigger about the durability of corpses. In captivity, up to thirty years, is the unexpected reply. (Are they good years? I want to ask, looking at the cages.) In the wild, maybe one year.

In books, and in our imaginations and dreams, snakes live forever. Images— photographs or the color plates in a field guide to snakes—are helpful, but images are no match for icons. The little Minoan goddess clutching a snake in either fist; the monsters of *Ragnarok* or *Anaconda*— such snake iterations barely need story lines attached to them (and a good thing too, since the plots of films like *Anaconda* don't stand up to narratological analysis). They have their own wordless eloquence. Neither do snakes weaving in and out of poems carry stories with them; rather, they appear and vanish and leave an aftertaste, whether Dickinson's zero at the bone or Lawrence's sense of his own pettiness.

Yet stories can coil around our snake sightings. The ancestral snake Curt and I are at once remembering and making up as we go along offers a way of conjuring back our father and brother, both now dead, at a time when they were much younger than Curt and I are now. People grow old and forget and die, but the grass and the well haven't changed much. And the plaid snake hasn't aged at all.

INVISIBILITY

It was a couple of months after moving my husband into a dementia facility that I first noticed it. The occasion was a concert of new music, the first such concert I'd attended in a long time. One of the composers whose work was being performed had known George; they'd been in graduate school together. The soprano had sung some of his musical settings, and it was she who had commissioned a piece, a setting of Whitman's "This Compost," which George had toiled on for a whole summer, pretty late in the period when he was still able to compose, and which she had then rejected as too difficult to learn.

At the reception after the concert, I knew who these people were—their names, their faces. Not that such recognition is tantamount to knowing someone. Still, my knowledge of them trumped theirs of me; the composer and the soprano didn't know who I was. Nor, which is not the same thing, did they realize that I recognized them.

The sensation, one with which I was to become very familiar, was of invisibility. You feel transparent, insubstantial, a non-person, at once intruder and also possibly voyeur, in the sense that you are observing people who do not know they're being watched for the simple reason that they can't see you. One reaction is to want to make them see you. That reception was the first time (far from the last time) I remember experiencing the Ancient Mariner's impulse to cross the room, buttonhole some hapless person heading toward the buffet table (wedding guest, concert-goer, the principle is the same), and tell my sad story. Or no, my husband's sad story— which was which? I resisted the impulse, and it passed.

As months turned into years, my cloak of invisibility showed no sign of vanishing. Sometimes, as at that post-concert reception, I would notice its presence in a crowded room. More often, though, I'd be on Broadway doing errands. Walking to the bank or the farmers' market or stepping out of a grocery store, I'd look up and recognize one of George's former colleagues. Sometimes it seemed to happen several times a week. As I stepped out the door of the Garden of Eden market, X would go by, heading north on Broadway, talking animatedly to his wife. As I paid for my of jar of honey and dozen eggs at the farmers' market, I'd see Y fingering apples at the next stand. As I chose a bunch of broccoli rabe in the crowded produce aisle of West Side Market, Z would be peering at the parsley and dill. Once I saw Z in profile (I think it was he) eating Sunday brunch, talking to a man whose profile I didn't recognize, sitting at a window table at Cafe du Soleil. Then for a while these non-encounters would abate.

Of course on any such occasion I could have made my presence known. But when I imagined the short, awkward conversations that would have been likely to ensue, conversations whose power to irk me would almost certainly be out of all proportion to their length, I always made the same swift choice: leave it. Let it go. What would they have said? What would I have said? Besides, I felt too proud, maybe too safe, to hail them from the impregnable disguise of my transparency. I wasn't alone there in the realm of the invisible; I had company, having often seen the dead walking along Broadway—my mother, for one, who died in 1992, and the poet Rachel Wetzsteon, who took her own life at the end of 2009. I've sometimes seen my husband, who isn't dead, not exactly, striding along. Perhaps I'd caught the condition from my husband, who while he was still living at home, still stalking around the neighborhood and taking daily walks in the park, had become—it's hard to explain, but those versed in dementia will know what I mean—invisible in plain sight.

With variations, the pattern of my invisibility continues. One more instance: recently, waiting for the light to change as I walked south on West End Avenue, I saw P cross from the east side to the west side of the street. This short man, who was walking a suitably miniature dog, wasn't one of George's former colleagues. He was someone I'd known since high school and had always liked; someone, moreover, who had been very kind when, back in 2005, I had sent friends an impossibly naive and hopeful letter to explain George's illness. That is, he'd actually answered the letter.

Of course it was sheer chance that I saw P and he didn't see me; he was in my sightline and I wasn't in his. I could easily have hailed him, and I almost did. Another day I probably would have. But I knew that the sight of me would elicit apologies and explanations. Having known P for so long, I knew that he tended to blame himself for things, to be, or at least to sound, contrite, and I had no wish either to add to his burdens or to reassure him that everything was fine. I let the moment go, and he crossed the street with his little dog.

Avoiding unsatisfactory conversations didn't keep me from brooding. Various possibilities presented themselves. Were these people pretending not to see me? I don't think so; I think they were just preoccupied by their own lives ("And they, since they/ Were not the one dead, turned to their affairs," as Frost puts it at the end of "Out, Out—"). Or was it perhaps the encroaching invisibility that shrouds women of a certain age that was affecting me, rather than anything to do with my husband? That wasn't out of the question, but was still too simple an explanation.

Puzzling at this conundrum, and beginning with a glimpse of the couple I've mentioned above, walking along talking to each other, I wrote this:

The Cloak

Quisque suos patimur manes

They might be any happy couple
except I happen to know them.
How do I know they're happy?
He's chuckling, turning toward her
as they hurry north on windy Broadway.
From under her fur hat she smiles at him.

Spell, curse, or blessing, the by now familiar
law operates: I see them,
they do not see me.
Color of bruise and shadow,
the cloak of invisibility
settles over my shoulders.

The afterlife turns out to be not quite
an afterlife. I am alive; I live there.
I step over the threshold
into a penumbral zone. I move
from solitude into a ghostly precinct,
a place of dimness, of transparency.

I'm stepping out the door of the Garden of Eden
as they stride past. Obedient to the law,
they do not see me. They are carrying
bags of provisions back to the apartment
they will unlock, go in, put down their bundles,
take off their coats, and shut the door behind them.

In one of those uncanny coincidences that seem most frequent when life presses in on us, I happened, not long after writing "The Cloak," upon a poem by Edward Thomas entitled "What Will They Do?" This poem, though I can't claim to understand it completely, seems to have been inspired at least in part by a somewhat similar experience of perceived invisibility.

What Will They Do?

What will they do when I am gone? It is plain
That they can do without me as the rain
Can do without the flowers and the grass

That profit by it and must perish without.
I have but seen them in the loud street pass;
And I was naught to them. I turned about
To see them disappearing carelessly.
But what if I in them as they in me
Nourished what has great value and no price?
Almost I thought that rain thirsts for a draught
Which only in the blossoms' chalice lies,
Until that one turned back and lightly laughed.

In her *Notes to The Annotated Poems of Edward Thomas*, editor Edna Longley comments that Thomas "often suffered from the paranoid belief that he was less visible or necessary to other people than they to him ... he was perversely pleased when the changes effected in his appearance by the army confirmed this: 'Nobody recognizes me now. Sturge Moore, Edward Marsh, & R. C. Trevelyan stood a yard off and I didn't trouble to awake them to stupid recognition.'"

Was Thomas's belief really all that paranoid? I suspect that Edward Thomas and I are not the only poets, or the only people, to have felt invisible. On the contrary, I've come to feel that it is probably a universal experience. I've also had occasion to remember that several of my poems that have nothing to do with George's illness are about crossings or farewells, encounters in which one person fleetingly but significantly sees another one: "The Red Hat" (1994), for example, where our son walks to school alone up West End Avenue and George and I turn back home; or "The Golden Road" (2009), in which my now grown son and I, having walked in opposite directions on a country road, encounter one another before going our separate ways. Frost captures a related feeling at the end of his poem "Meeting and Passing": "Afterward I went past what you had passed/ Before we met and you what I had passed."

And there's more to say about this ghostly realm. For that invisibility is akin to ghostliness is something I must have known without knowing I knew it, when I chose the epigraph to "The Cloak": *Quisque suos patimur manes.* This darkly luminous phrase is from the sixth book of the *Aeneid*. Anchises, in the underworld, is explaining to Aeneas what happens to souls after death.

My recent path back to Vergil had been an unexpected one. Last Christmas, my son gave me Ursula LeGuin's latest novel, *Lavinia*. I'd already read it (not that I told him so at the time), but now I reread the book, slowly and with more relish. In this novel LeGuin attempts with a measure of success to give a voice and personality to her eponymous heroine, that figure who in the *Aeneid* comes across as shadowy and faceless, a plot device rather than a character.

The eerie scenes early in the novel where Lavinia converses with the poet Vergil—or rather with his emanation (for of course Vergil lived centuries after the character he created)—are, provided one can suspend disbelief, among the book's most evocative. One passage among these improbable conversations that I kept coming back to quotes, in translation, the mysterious phrase I've already referred to. Lavinia is thinking about her twilit colloquies with the poet who will immortalize her (or at least her name) centuries hence:

No doubt I will eventually fade away and be lost in oblivion, as I would have done long ago if the poet hadn't summoned me into existence. Perhaps I will become a false dream clinging like a bat to the underside of the leaves of the tree at the gate of the underworld. . . . But I won't have to tear myself from life and go down into the dark, as he did, poor man, first in his imagination, and then as his own ghost. We each have to endure our own afterlife, he said to me once, or that is one way to understand what he said.

We each have to endure our own *afterlife*. Although I hadn't looked at the Aeneid in Latin for many years, I was somehow able to summon up the words from its sixth book, the words I knew LeGuin was thinking of: *quisque suos patimur manes*. The phrase was a natural epigraph for my poem "The Cloak," which I was working on at about this time, because it seems to refer to both survival and ghosts: to what happens after we die. To Aeneas's plaintive question to his father in the underworld, when he asks "Father, do some souls really soar back skyward/ From here, returning into sluggish bodies?/ What dreadful longing sends them toward the light?" I quote only part of Anchises's magnificent long answer, with its Pythagorean and Lucretian overtones:

> But when, on the last day, a life departs,
> Not every evil sickness of the body
> Wholly withdraws from the poor spirit—many
> Are long grown in, mysteriously ingrained.
> So souls are disciplined and pay the price
> Of old wrongdoing. Some are splayed, exposed

To hollow winds; a flood submerges some,
Washing out wickedness; fire scorches some pure.
Each bears his own ghosts, then a few are sent
To live in broad Elysium's happy fields,
Till Time's great circle is completed. . . .

(*Aeneid* VI 735-45, translated by Sarah Ruden)

Quisque suos patimur manes. Ruden renders it "Each bears his own ghosts"; LeGuin qualifies this recognition: "We each have to endure our own afterlife ... or that is one way to understand what he said." Here are a handful of other ways the phrase has been rendered: "All have their Manes, and those Manes bear" (Dryden, 1697); "We all endure/ Our ghostly retribution" (Christopher Pearse Cranch, 1872); "Each our own shade-correction we endure" (T. H. Delabere-May, 19th c.); "Each of us finds in the next world his own level" (Cecil Day Lewis, 1952); "First each of us must suffer his own shade" (Allen Mandelbaum, 1961); "We each suffer his own shade" (Robert Fitzgerald, 1981); "Each of us must suffer his own demanding ghost" (Robert Fagles, 2006).

I love the ambiguities here. There is a suggestion of punishment, a punishment that seems not only earned—just, purgative punishment—but also reflexive. Are we not our own ghosts, or rather, are they not us? What we suffer is the consequence of ghostliness. And ghostliness brings me back to the invisibility I started from. What is invisibility if not ghostliness? There are other ghosts in this vicinity as well, too many to count. Dementia—especially when it is linked, as George's is, to aphasia—

is a guaranteed purveyor of ghostliness. I also think of what the dying Keats referred to as his own posthumous existence. Looping back to Vergil, I think of Aeneas carrying his father on his shoulders out of the ruins of Troy. It seems to me I've been carrying George for years now; even though he isn't at home any longer, I am still carrying him. The people I have met in the past year and a half, people whose husbands and wives and partners live in the same place that George does, are similarly carrying ghosts on their shoulders. To each his own, her own: *quisque suos patimur manes.* If there is also some sense of karmic pattern here, as in the Buddhist notion that all beings are owners of and heirs to their own actions—well, the Vergilian phrase, however we construe it, clearly encompasses that, too. Did George do something to deserve this ghostliness? Did I? "So souls are disciplined and pay the price/ Of old wrongdoing."

Invisibility puts you in an uncanny position, but it's a position I'm getting used to. Seen from one point of view, it offers a safe vantage point: you have a good view, plus you're uncapturable. But it can also be drafty and chilly and lonely. One meaning of *quisque suos patimur manes* is surely that—in certain circumstances, anyway—each of us becomes a peculiar kind of ghost. We may feel like flesh and blood, but if we're invisible to other people, then maybe that feeling is an illusion.

We teeter uneasily between worlds. The anthropologist Michael Jackson, who seems to live in a constant state of transit and transition, has recently written a book entitled *The Palm at the End of the Mind.* Although he writes and quotes poetry, and although his title suggests that he feels some sense of kinship with Wallace Stevens, Jackson isn't primarily a poet but a student of human behavior. When he uses words like "liminal," "penumbral," and "border," I know he is in ghostly—which is to say, familiar—territory; as a denizen of some kind of border zone myself, I pay attention. When Jackson asserts that "border situations not only imply a radical break from the known; they presage new possibilities of relatedness … the human capacity for forming bonds knows no bounds," I recognize the truth of his words and I take heart.

Jackson observes, perhaps evoking Wordsworth, "all new life requires a death, even if this death is only a forgetting." Beginnings do require endings. The other spouses at George's facility have begun to fill a space in my life that started emptying out years ago, when George's colleagues ceased to see me. The human capacity for forming new bonds is predicated on the loosening of old bonds. How confusing, then, that these old bonds continue to tug at me, no matter how loose some of them appear to have become.

I've reached some kind of balance, poised between old bonds and new. The ghost's invisibility is contagious, so I've now become a little transparent myself, and I keep carrying a burden whose weight I often no longer notice. I bear my own ghost. When I visit George in his realm of aphasia, our two ghosts converse together, without words, but not without feeling.

THE MISSING MOTHER

We were looking at Michael's new poem. It was about having breakfast with his father in a diner, and thus belonged to what seemed to be emerging as a series of family poems in which no mother figured. "Why is your mother not at the diner with you in this poem?" a less than tactful student in the workshop asked. Since part of Michael's poetic landscape was, in addition to diner settings, precisely this absence of a mother, the rest of us around the table stifled sighs. Not that anyone knew the entire answer to the question. I had had one conversation with Michael back in September and had learned something of his complicated family background, but there was much more that I didn't know. Still, some questions shouldn't be asked.

Before the seminar ended, ten or fifteen minutes were left over for free writing. Here's how this works: I bring in a sheaf of images (postcards or other images of works of art or photographs) and ask the students to choose one image, keep it in front of them on the table, and write without stopping for ten minutes, if not necessarily about the image, then in response to it.

Once they had picked out their images, the students

wrote with the charged attention this exercise always seems to elicit. I prowled around the table, looking over people's shoulders to see who was writing about what. The tactless questioner had chosen a photograph of a small seated bronze Buddha. Elizabeth had a pen-and-ink Rembrandt drawing of a woman in a bedroom; Roberto had a Blake image of figures symmetrically flanked by monsters. Michael had picked out a reproduction of a Picasso drawing. I had cut this image out of a Frick Museum publication; a show of early Picasso was currently on display at the museum. "About the size of a dollar bill" is how Elizabeth Bishop describes a painting in "Poem." The image Michael was studying wasn't much bigger than a large postage stamp. I know how small that reproduction of the Picasso drawing is, since I later retrieved the image and taped it to a folder.

So there, in Picasso's delicate rendering, was the missing mother. A thin young woman, head cocked to one side, tenderly cradles an infant in her arms, gazing down at it with that maternal absorption for which "intense" is far too pale a word. The baby reaches up a hand to touch the mother's cheek. Near the margins of the page, an extra, larger right hand or two are carefully sketched, as if the artist is practicing his execution. Nature needs time and space to replicate; art can snatch any available corner of the page and make use of it.

It is possible that Michael hadn't known his mother was missing until he happened to be confronted with this representation—possible, although the aching absence in many of his poems makes it seem unlikely. Possibly he'd been looking for his mother for years, perhaps without knowing what it was he was searching for. It might not have occurred to him that he was in quest of a mother until he noticed her absence peering at him from the mirror of the diner where he and his father were, not for the first time, having breakfast. His poem eloquently evokes the companionable silence of father and son: "Out of politeness, we open our menus / but we know what we want."

Who could have guessed that the drawing of a young mother and her child would spill out of the battered manila envelope I'd barely remembered to bring to class and land almost in Michael's lap? Maybe the mother had been lost, but here, surely, was a replacement. It often happens when we are young, and even when we're not so young, that until we see our wants and needs depicted, we barely know what they are. We're conscious of an appetite or an anguish or an ache, but why and for what or whom? With his signature mixture of precision and bluntness, Primo Levi wrote a passage I stumbled upon around the same time Michael and the Picasso drawing found one another: "Anguish is known to everyone since childhood and everyone knows that it is often blank, undifferentiated. It rarely carries a clearly written label that also contains its motivation; when it does have one, it is often mendacious. One can believe or declare oneself to be anguished for one reason and be so due to something totally different; one can think that one is suffering at facing the future and instead be suffering because of one's past; one can think that one is suffering for others, out of pity, out of compassion, and instead be suffering for one's own reasons, more or less profound, more or less avowable and avowed; sometimes so deep that only the specialist, the analyst of souls, knows how to exhume them."

The analyst of souls, or the artist, or the poet. When my father died, I was seventeen years old. I grieved and knew that I was grieving, but my recollection is that I didn't clearly register the depth of the hollow I was carrying around until someone else noticed my loss—someone I knew well, a poet I was seeing in the months after my father's death. Years later, I was to find that poems written centuries earlier can speak to what we're feeling this moment; writers long dead can miraculously express and so assuage the pain of the living. But in 1967, it provided an unexpected validation of my grief to read, in a poem X wrote about his and my respective troubles, the line "the lost father submerged among the living." So my pain wasn't only private; it came across to someone who knew me, someone not in my small family, where we each—my mother and sister and I—bore our bereavement in a different way. The poem expressed, in that one line, the way our beloved dead blur and merge with those who populate our lives. We stumble upon our losses at every turn, but at every turn we also seem to find their images "among the living," and we often misapprehend the living in the process.

Much of X's poem, the title of which I don't recall, was about his own troubles, notably his failing marriage. The poem ends by heading underwater, perhaps to that same place where my loss was submerged. It asks "Are we the two fish of my dream?" He fresh from his loss, I from mine—perhaps we could swim together for a while. As indeed, for a few months, we did.

That affair is long over. My father died many years ago. And yet the sympathetic insight of that single luminous line brings back the young man who wrote it, the sad adolescent who was me, and the winter months in Cambridge when we were seeing each other. It also brings back the loss that was so new then, and that has since grown into my personality as a strand of wire grows into the bark of a tree. The poem Michael began to write as he stared at that Picasso drawing was written in the first person. The voice was that of a mother nursing her child for the first time.

Nothing's Mortal Enemy

I see from the flyleaf of my copy of Daniel Schacter's *The Seven Sins of Memory* that I bought the book in July, 2001. This was fairly early in the period when I knew (without acknowledging to myself that I knew it) that there was something wrong with my husband, and that the problem had to do with memory. The "sins" Schacter anatomizes in his engaging study do not include dementia; rather, he articulates and clarifies various memory problems for the worried well.

A few years passed; my worries intensified, with good reason, as George's cognitive and behavioral problems increased. In 2004, he was unable to finish the fall semester at Columbia University, where he had long taught in the Music Department; early in 2005 he was diagnosed with a dementia. In October, 2011, he died. And it was about a month after his death that I picked up Schacter's book again. I remembered that the last memory "sin" Schacter discusses is the opposite of a memory deficit; rather, it is the persistence of unwanted memories. George's last few months had been turbulent, rife with 911 calls, emergency rooms, and expulsions from facilities; and I found by Thanksgiving that I was having some unsettlingly vivid memories of what had happened between June and October.

Schacter's notion of "the sin of persistence" proved to be both reassuring and useful. However searing my memories of those last months were, they didn't threaten to unseat my sense of who I was, and that realization was reassuring. More important, Schacter's book was useful because it pointed me (as it hadn't on my first reading in 2001) to the fascinating work on memory by British clinical psychologist and suicide expert Mark Williams. In his book *Cry of Pain*, Williams explores how some depressed people tend to have very vague and general memories. Predictably, they find positive memories hard to retrieve; but more unexpectedly, the more depressed the individuals Williams studied were, the more trouble they seemed to have pulling up any specific memories, whether positive or negative. Rather, their memories tended to be what Williams calls generic.

Once the difficult span of George's long illness was over, it seemed important to pay attention to my own well-being. Would the burden I had carried for so long take its toll now that I had, or thought I had, put it down? These were the questions that had led me back to Schacter and thence to Williams. Their work made the very vividness of my memories begin to look more advantageous than otherwise. Rather than a bleak, undifferentiated landscape or narrative, I was dealing with an unruly embarrassment of riches. True, I remembered 911 calls and ambulance rides and emergency rooms. But I also remembered Father Flynn, the priest in one nursing home whom I mistook for a chaplain before being told he was a resident, who was unfailingly kind to George. I remembered the countless aides and nurses who worked with George along the way (their faces if not all their names), and I remembered the doctors, who still walk kindly through my dreams. I remembered the river views from the eighth floor of Milstein Pavilion at Columbia-Presbyterian, where George spent so many weeks in June, August, and September. The earthquake of August 22, 2011, and Hurricane Irene were events I experienced at Milstein. Every place where George lived or even passed through, and there were many, came with its own associations; every person I met was nested in their own story. How could I forget?

Throughout George's illness, I had cultivated memory. In my memoir *Strange Relation*, which was published nine months before George's death, I discuss how reading and writing helped me to understand what was going on:

Though many of them are certainly beautiful, [the books I had been reading] didn't soothe or console or lull me with their beauty. On the contrary, they made me sit up and pay attention. Each in its own way, they helped me by telling me the truth, or rather a truth, about the almost overwhelming situation in which I found myself...If silence was the enemy, literature was my best friend. No matter how lonely, frightened, confused, or angry I felt, some writer had captured the sensation...And

I could write...I rediscovered what every writing teacher knows, that writing what you remember helps you to remember more...The more I wrote, the more I remembered and understood.

In the light of my lifelong habit of using writing to understand and express what I was feeling, it's clear that I had long intuitively understood and acted on the principle that Schacter spells out when he writes: "Disclosing difficult experiences to others...can have profoundly positive effects." Schacter alludes to a study showing the benefits associated with "the act of converting turbulent emotions into narrative form"—a result that would hardly come as news to Rita Charon, or Arthur Frank, or Ann Burack-Weiss, or any of the growing number of physicians, social workers, and writers associated with the narrative medicine movement.

Whether its genre is narrative or poetic, the tasks literature performs, and the benefits it confers, turn out to be remarkably close to the positive effects of Williams's "emotional processing," the dynamic which "involves being able to return voluntarily to specific details of events, sometimes to give a greater sense of control over them, sometimes to generate alternative explanations or accounts of them." Precisely these abilities—to revisit, to turn over in one's mind so as to see from a fresh angle, to re-conceptualize, to revisit the unfolding narrative—were important to me during George's illness and are no less crucial now that his death has shifted the landscape.

Poetry is my chosen genre, or rather the genre that

long ago chose me. And poetry's gift of figuration and trope is an important ingredient of my own emotional processing. I envision invisible things such as an illness or an emotion by likening them to something else. As Theseus puts it in *A Midsummer Night's Dream*, the poet "gives to airy nothings / A local habitation and a name." When something amorphous and elusive takes on a shape, I can understand and remember it better; and I am then free to change that shape.

In my experience, therefore, Susan Sontag's magisterial and influential insistence in *Illness as Metaphor* that "the most truthful way of regarding illness...is one most purified of, most resistant to, metaphoric thinking" is unhelpful and untrue. Sontag's is a laudable goal: she wants people to stop blaming themselves and others for illnesses. But the understanding of both human nature and the nature of language that underlies her dictum seems flawed.

Let me end by suggesting a more realistic and useful view of the incorrigible human tendency to liken one thing to another. My source here is James Merrill (1926—95), a great poet who was wise in the ways of human behavior as well as poetry. Unlike Sontag, Merrill doesn't lay down the law. Instead, in a sonnet embedded in his long poem *Mirabell: Books of Number*, Merrill makes an astute comment and asks a salient question: "It's hopeless, the way people try / To avoid the sentimental fallacy— / How can a person not personify?" Later in the poem, which is really a compact essay on poetics, he writes "Putting it into words / Means also that it puts words into me.../

And I am nothing's mortal enemy, / Surrendered, by the white page, to the scene."

It isn't only the writer who is "nothing's mortal enemy," it is poetry itself which fights against oblivion and silence. Every writing teacher knows that the very process of writing generates further ideas and memories and perceptions. To this fertile dynamic, poetry adds a couple of extra benefits. Its use of trope helps to make the world vivid and meaningful while also encouraging each reader to supply her own associations. Thus Constantine Cavafy's rich little poem "Walls" will have different meanings for different readers, but the poem's halo of connotation means that it inevitably suggests more than literal walls. Thomas Hardy's "The Subalterns" personifies wind, sky, illness, and death so that these forces can speak to the agonized questions the poem implies. In addition, such poetic elements as rhythm and rhyme can help make poems effective mnemonic devices, utterances "lodged," in Robert Frost's words, "where they are hard to get rid of."

Late in George's illness, when he was almost completely mute, conversation was impossible. But I was able to read him poems he had loved, some of which he had set to music—poems by Gerard Manley Hopkins or George Herbert or Walt Whitman. Poetry filled the silence incomparably better than unilateral small talk about sports or politics. "The Flower," "Spring and Fall," "This Compost"—all are meditations on much more than a plant or a season, all take the natural world as their starting point for rich reflections on time, cycles, life, death.

Nothing's mortal enemy. Contrast this humane and courageous notion with the desolate worlds almost bare of image and narrative conjured up by the people with severe depression Williams describes, who were unable to retrieve details from their own pasts that might have been helpful in building more hopeful futures. Contrast it as well with Sontag's censorious austerity, which assumes that metaphor is some kind of decadent ornament instead of our psychological birthright. Inundated by memories of my husband's long illness, I am indeed nothing's mortal enemy. Like so much in poetry, the phrase has more than one meaning. I am pitted against blankness; and perhaps I am also the friend of everything—even of the memories of those last months.

ATTENTION

I turn the page; turn back; read it again, slowly. This poem, "Museum" by Jay Rogoff, has something to say to me about concentration. Poems about painting often admonish us to be more attentive; they're about looking or trying to look, with all that action's attendant distractions and digressions. Rogoff, charmingly, even loopily self-aware, watches himself in a museum watching a young woman who looks like a Degas dancer studying a Degas painting of a dancer. Finally, whether because she feels his gaze or because she has come to the end of her own attention, she leaves the room and vanishes "into the next gallery."

What do the gazer and the two dancers (live and painted), or alternatively the two gazers and the painting, have to do with me? A poem can console you if you let it; one often needs consolation. It can transport you—Emily Dickinson's "prancing poetry"—we often need such transportation. Poems can't accomplish this all the time, of course; nor can all poems be expected to teleport their readers into another realm. Nevertheless, the tantalizing possibility always clings about the genre.

Recently, I edited an anthology, the second in a series

called *The Waiting Room Reader*. The idea behind it is that these collections of poetry and short prose be made available in doctors' waiting rooms across the country. Is the intention to distract? To console? To console by distracting? The essential task of the book, I decided, was not so much consolation or distraction as simply the fostering of attention: "In circumstances where we can do little but just be there, it helps to pay attention to something," I wrote in my preface. "Paying attention to one particular thing, rather, than flipping pages or scrolling text, prevents us from being distracted and thus, paradoxically, can successfully distract us—can move our minds, if only briefly, from the claustrophobic space and the repetitive scenarios in which we may feel trapped."

The Waiting Room Reader was based on an idea that was far from new to me: bring something to read while you're waiting. This was my crutch throughout the years of my husband's illness, and it remains useful. Keats and Kafka, I remember, kept me company one winter day about a dozen years ago when I was donating platelets and was tethered to a slow machine in the basement of Citicorp. Earlier still, when my friend Charles Barber was dying of AIDS, I read him the first chapter of my much-annotated teaching copy of *Emma*, which I happened to be carrying. As it turned out, there would be no time for further chapters, but Charlie enjoyed hearing that one. "I see," he said. "Highbury opens like a fan." One black December night a few years later, before I caught a taxi to meet my husband and his helper in the emergency room at Columbia-Presbyterian hospital, I flung an apple, a cookie, a bottle of water, and a book that had just come in the mail that day into my shoulder bag—it happened to be David Slavitt's translation of *Orlando Furioso.* Serendipity certainly plays a role. And of course one does not always have the time or inclination, or even the physical space, to read.

When I was considering submissions for the second volume of *The Waiting Room Reader* (the purpose of the anthology had been advertised and poems poured in), I realized I wasn't after narratives (which you get in newspapers or magazines) or conversations (which you get in telephone or texting exchanges); I wanted nouns. I found myself drawn to poems that memorably presented things: a scar, a sweater, a bird's nest, a dog. But poems function like verbs, too. All the poems in this collection turned out, one way or another, to recall, to evoke, to praise; all seemed to be acts of reclamation. The same goes for Jay Rogoff's "Museum," a poem which triply observes and celebrates (in an expansive use of the second person which also embraces the reader) the goofy speaker/gazer, the absorbed young woman, and the painting they are both studying: "you haul / your attention back to the work / of art from the work / of art. Yes. / Yes the forms." Those forms—of dance, of painting, of poetry—have an eternal, Platonic quality which in its serenity and austerity can be, if not precisely consoling, then at least steadying.

Nor is it only the forms of art which steady us as we wait. The "one particular thing," paying attention to which, as I wrote, can distract us when we need to be distracted, is whatever is available. It might not be a poem or a painting. The Greek poet Yannis Ritsos, interned on one prison island or another in the late 1940s and early 50s, wrote poems recording his experiences in these bleak settings. Beautifully edited and translated by Karen Emmerich and Edmund Keeley as *Diaries of Exile*, his journal-like verses record soccer games, meals, the late arrival of newspapers, moonlight, sheep bells. But that's not all. There is a scoured, chastened, slowed-down quality of abstraction to the poem I happened to flip to because it was written on the day I was born, November 8, 1948:

Bit by bit the leaves on the grape vine turned yellow.
Now they're brown and red.
The wind blows through them in the afternoon. We struggle
to bind our attention to a color a stone
the way an ant walks. A bumblebee
creeping along a dry leaf makes as much noise
as a passing tram. That's how we realize
what silence has settled within us.

"The way an ant walks" sent me back to a poem I wrote in a moment of waiting when I had not a book but a notebook that doubled as a sketchpad on my knee: "I bend to the open notebook; distracted, turn my head. / Tiny brown ants are climbing up a stalk of golden-rod. / It isn't clear what goal they hope to reach." "Only So Much," the title of my poem, refers to attention: "There is only so much we can notice all at once." How much attention can we summon at will? "We struggle to bind our attention to the way an ant walks," writes Ritsos. Where else would his attention, or mine, wander off to? James Merrill's "Time," a work that moves between verse and prose, fixes on the symptoms of the poem's addressee, a friend suffering from an inability to focus attention for long on anything, including finishing the letter he is writing.

You swiftly wrote:

> "... this long silence. I don't know what's the matter with me. All winter I have been trying to discipline myself—'Empty the mind', as they say in the handbooks, 'concentrate on one thing, any thing, the snowflake, the granite it falls upon, the planet risen opposite, etc, etc'—and failing, failing. Quicksands of leisure!" ...

The pen reels from your hand.

"Quicksands of leisure" elegantly evokes the abundance of empty time to be found in a surprising number of venues from waiting rooms to rocks in Vermont fields to the island of Leros. The silence and the emptiness are waiting for us. The open notebook may beckon, or we may drop our pen. If we have a book to read, so much the better. But first it seems necessary to face the blankness of the page or the sky—to feel, as Ritsos puts it, the silence settling within us.

Mortal Beauty

I.

By far the pleasantest place at Hearthstone, the dementia facility in White Plains, was the rooftop garden, where I could sit with George when the days got sunny. Having moved him to Hearthstone early in January, I learned by early spring to bring bubble stuff or a ball or a Frisbee to play with when I visited, as well as some food and maybe a little wine or a bottle of beer, so we could have a picnic at the table on the patio. But despite these stabs at pleasant ways of passing time, what chiefly stays with me from the eight months George spent at Hearthstone, between January and August 2008, is a sense of dread. Wracked by guilt at having moved him out of our apartment, I was afraid for all those months to talk to him about anything, like the cats, that might remind him of home. So I was reduced to talking about politics or sports or weather—a feeble parody of small talk. In retrospect, it didn't help that George could—barely—still talk at that time. His room at Hearthstone was big—too big. The room was a double; its other bed was, except for a brief and disastrous interlude, unoccupied. It was bright and sunny. But there was nothing to do in it.

Nor did it help that I hardly ever seemed to see other visiting families. Occasionally I'd encounter someone in the elevator who was riding up, as I was, to the fifth floor. To press the button to this dementia floor required a special key. We visitors might exchange an apologetic, almost guilty smile, perhaps a hasty word or two, and that was it.

Around Memorial Day 2008, several things happened. George assaulted the man who was briefly his roommate; as a result, he was hospitalized in the psychiatric ward of the local hospital. A woman named Ruth chanced to be in this hospital at the same time, and she and George were discharged to Hearthstone more or less together— he to return, she to move in. Ruth had been living with her husband in the Esplanade, the assisted living facility of which Hearthstone (the dementia ward) occupied one floor, and the decision had evidently been made to move her to Hearthstone. After she moved, her husband, who remained in their old apartment, visited Ruth every day.

White-haired and frail, Ruth was clearly much older than George, who was then sixty-five (he looked younger). And what one prays for in such situations happened: George and Ruth made friends. From what I could see when I visited, he seemed protective of her, taking her arm as they walked up and down the rooftop patio, or just sitting near her in the dining room. They didn't talk much. More likely they didn't talk at all.

Though I couldn't know it at the time, the visit to Hearthstone I'm thinking of now—the visit I remember, and want to remember, the most clearly—was one of my last. It was late spring or early summer. George and I had left his room and, as the layout of the place dictated, we were passing through the dining area on our way to the terrace. At one of the tables, George halted. Ruth was sitting there alone: silent, sunken into herself, starting out at nothing. From his height of nearly six feet four, George looked down at her, and laid a gentle hand on her shoulder. Ruth put both her hands up on George's hand while it still rested on her shoulder, and cupped his hand between hers. Then she brought his hand—still sandwiched between both of hers—over to her lips and kissed it. Not one word was said by either of them.

I was there, standing by George's side, not in a hurry, ready to pause when he paused. I chanced to look at Ruth at the right moment, and so happened to take the whole vignette in. But this silent little scene would have been very easy to miss. It was over in less than a minute. George and I made our way to the sunny terrace and the visit continued.

I think I would have remembered this poignant tableau without any help. But the sight of Ruth and George's mute affection was so striking that it jarred loose a couple of poems from my memory, poems which seemed to encapsulate several themes swirling around like dustmotes in the spring sunlight that day. These themes included old age, mutability, and beauty. Beauty is fleeting, ephemeral —so how to hold onto it? How even to notice it? Is it best to focus on it purposefully or to catch it in passing? Yet elusive as it is, beauty can make its presence unmistakably felt. In that moment Ruth and George shared, beauty was there.

II.

One of George's favorite poets had always been Gerard Manley Hopkins, several of whose poems he set to music: "The Blessed Virgin Compared to the Air We Breathe," "At the Wedding March," "Of Nature as a Heraclitean Fire," "Pied Beauty," "Heaven-Haven," "Spelt from Sibyl's Leaves," and "The Leaden Echo and the Golden Echo." But when I think about George's hand between Ruth's hands, and Ruth raising his hand to her lips and kissing it, the Hopkins poem that comes to mind is one that George knew but never set, a sonnet entitled "To What Serves Mortal Beauty?" At least I think George knew it—I have an inchoate memory of the two of us sharing our delight in the poem's first line:

To what serves mortal beauty | - dangerous; does set dancing
blood -

Admittedly, this memory of shared pleasure in the poem could well be a fabrication. I do know I love those lines, which are the only lines in the poem I'm sure I understand. There are also other memories, joyful memories, related to George and Hopkins poems that

I'm positive are real rather than fictive. One of these
is my reading him "Pied Beauty" over and over in the
garden behind his family's Squirrel Island cottage in the
summer of 1977, so that he could get the poem into his
ear, preparatory to setting it for soprano and chamber
orchestra. Later that summer, in the house in Vermont,
he set the short lyric "Heaven-Haven" to music in a single
afternoon.

Heaven-Haven

(a nun takes the veil)

I have desired to go
         Where springs not fail,
To fields where flies no sharp and sided hail
    And a few lilies blow.

And I have asked to be
         Where no storms come,
Where the green swell is in the havens dumb,
    And out of the swing of the sea.

Fast-forward thirty-odd years. It's the end of summer
2010, and I am alone in the same house in Vermont. My
sister's visit has come and gone; my son is traveling
in India with his girlfriend; George is in a facility in
Manhattan. I am learning to fill this space alone. The
silence, full of memories and echoes and tranquility, is
good for poetry: writing it, reading it, hearing it in my
head. One of the poems I hear is "Mortal Beauty," but I
can't remember the poem very well; it's time to reread

it. And when I go over to the shelf and pull out the small Penguin paperback, W.H. Gardner's edition of Hopkins's selected poetry and prose, a surprise awaits me. This is the very book George consulted when he set Hopkins's poems to music. Here are the jotted notes in the margin in his handwriting.

I sit down on the sofa with the book in my lap. What a trove has been patiently waiting on the bookshelf here in this summer house, weathering long freezing winters and years of neglect! I feel as if I am simultaneously discovering a valuable, hitherto unknown document and recovering a cherished letter that I'd assumed was lost. My initial sense of surprise and gratitude doesn't even take into account the beauty of the poems in these pages. But here the poems are, intricate, delicate, and powerful (all adjectives I would apply to George's music), all bringing home to me once again who my husband was, what he lost, what I lost, and what remains.

So much remains. In a phrase of Robert Frost, the wonder of unexpected supply keeps growing. For example, before I turn to "Mortal Beauty" I stumble upon a poem I'd forgotten.

Moonrise June 19
1876

I awoke in the midsummer not-to-call night, | in the white and
    the walk of the morning:
The moon, dwindled and thinned to the fringe | of a fingernail
    héld to the cándle,
Or páring of páradisáïcal fruit, | lovely in wáning but lústreless,

Stepped from the stool, drew back from the barrow, | of dark
    Maenefa the mountain;
A cusp still clasped him, a fluke yet fanged him, | entangled
    him, not quit utterly.
This was the prized, the desirable sight, | unsought, presented
    so easily,
Parted me leaf and leaf, divided me, | eyelid and eyelid of
    slumber.

This is a poem George had set before we met, and
which we used to quote to one another on moonlit nights
in Vermont. When I wake up on moonlit nights there, I
still think of these lines. The poem brings back moonlit
nights when I was not alone.

And so much is lost. One way to think of George,
swathed as he now is in almost total silence, is that he
has taken a veil. The word "dumb" in "Heaven-Haven"
strikes a note that considering George's aphasia is eerily
prescient. Yet Hopkins's mysterious line (and I remember
how George made the music swell with "in the havens
dumb") is so rich that together with tenderness and pity
and sadness, I feel hope that my husband is now in a place
where no storms come.

As I page through the volume, other Hopkins poems
speak to me. They also speak to each other. Some of
them sound as if they are speaking for George. George
translated Hopkins's poetry into music; now that George
needs other voices to speak for him, this poetry is
translating his silence back into language.

All in Hopkins's distinctive idiolect, the poems I pause
over bear a strong family resemblance to one another.

Not only do they share a recognizable style, they also touch upon the same immense topics. "Mortal Beauty" worries at the same question asked and answered by "The Leaden Echo and the Golden Echo." Both poems, acknowledging the powerful presence of beauty, also see beauty as willful, problematic, and fugitive. What use is beauty? asks "Mortal Beauty." "How to keep back beauty from vanishing away?" is the burden of the Leaden Echo:

The Leaden Echo

How to kéep — is there ány any, is there none such, nowhere
    known some, bow or brooch or braid or brace, láce, latch
    or catch or key to keep
Back beauty, keep it, beauty, beauty, beauty,... from vanishing
    away?
Ó is there no frowning of these wrinkles, ránkèd wrinkles
    deep,
Dówn? no waving off of these most mournful messengers, still
    messengers, sad and stealing messengers of grey?
No there's none, there's none, O no there's none,
Nor can you long be, what you now are, called fair,
Do what you may do, what, do what you may,
And wisdom is early to despair:
Be beginning; since, no, nothing can be done
To keep at bay
Age and age's evils, hoar hair,
Ruck and wrinkle, drooping, dying, death's worst, winding
    sheets, tombs and worms and tumbling to decay;
So be beginning, be beginning to despair.
O there's none; no no no there's none:
Be beginning to despair, to despair,
Despair, despair, despair, despair.

Echoing the Leaden Echo's woeful final syllable, The

Golden Echo transforms despair into something hopeful:

Spare!
There ís one, yes I have one (Hush there!);
Only not within seeing of the sun.
Not within the singeing of the strong sun,
Tall sun's tingeing, or treacherous the tainting of the earth's
    air,
Somewhere elsewhere there is (ah well where!) one,
One. Yes I cán tell such a key, I dó know such a place,
Where whatever's prized and passes of us, everything that's
    fresh and fast flying of us, seems to us sweet of us and
    swiftly away with, done away with, undone,
Úndone, done with, soon done with, and yet dearly and
    dangerously sweet
Of us, the wimpled-water-dimpled, not-by-morning-matchéd
    face,
The flower of beauty, fleece of beauty, too too apt to, ah ! to
    fleet,
Never fleets móre, fastened with the tenderest truth
To its own best being and its loveliness of youth: it is an ever-
    lastingness of, O it is an all youth!

The pages I'm poring over now as I go back to
Hopkins's text, the pages George studied when he was
setting "The Leaden Echo and the Golden Echo," are
not only marked with penciled arrows, brackets, and
various other marginalia; they are also grubby with the
marks of George's fingers. Stained by pipe tobacco or
wood ash, those beautiful long fingers were often none
too clean. There is good news here: the physical traces
on the yellowing paper of this once extremely attentive
man's attention. There is bad news too, as I turn these
pages and try to think back through more than twenty

years to the last time George read these pages, marked them, used them—reading is too pale a verb. This bad news is of decay: "no, nothing can be done / to keep at bay / Age and age's evils, hoar hair, / Ruck and wrinkle, drooping dying…" George is sixty-seven now. His hair is barely frosted with grey and his face is unwrinkled. But even though for people who don't know him it isn't immediately obvious that he is unable to speak, it has gradually become apparent to anyone seeing his face, his walk, his whole aspect, that something is very wrong.

To what serves mortal beauty? That challenging question, a question that doesn't seem all that rhetorical, is not easy to answer. Hopkins immediately cautions us that mortal beauty is "dangerous." But then, without gainsaying this danger, he seems to take the reader by the hand and point out mortal beauty's use: "See: it does this; keeps warm / Men's wits to the things that are…" And he goes on to make a distinction both crucial and subtle between glancing at beauty and gazing at it, by which I take him to mean between happening to glimpse beauty and staring straight at it: "…a glance / master more may than gaze…"

III.

I happened to see beauty, to catch it on the wing, in that dining room in White Plains. I was definitely glancing and not gazing at the moment when I caught George putting his hand on Ruth's shoulder and Ruth taking his hand between hers, lifting it to her lips, and kissing it. That beauty in the dining room was no less real for being evanescent. And now there's the beauty of the poems on these pages I'm turning in my silent house—pages George marked with a pencil some thirty years ago.

"...beauty, keep it, beauty, beauty, beauty"—the echoing word turns into the trill of a bird song. As the sound repeats, the meaning gets lost.

In our daily lives, beauty is easy to miss. There are many reasons for this. As countless poetic variations on the *carpe diem* theme remind us, beauty doesn't stand still. It vanishes quickly from young faces and bodies. Or, sneakier, beauty hides in plain sight, so that we lumber right on past it, our gaze fixed on the next thing—for example, not on the dining room where Ruth, one old woman among others, sits motionless in her chair, but on the sunny terrace where we hope to go. If we don't pause at the right moment, we may well pass beauty by. Indeed, if beauty keeps our wits warm "to the things that are," it may also be that unless our wits are already warm, we won't register beauty on the wing. But there are no guarantees, no foolproof method of tracking and capturing beauty, for if we pause too long and purposefully to investigate, we may well also miss it. Stopping in a museum to stare at a statue or a painting may bring the beauty of the art into focus, or it may not. This is part of what Hopkins means when he writes that "a glance / Master more may than gaze."

Not only is beauty hard to locate, notice, or hold onto. It's hard to calibrate the flow of beauty in relation to our desires. How much of this fugitive stuff do we need? How much can we even bear? Take a simpler, a universal human need: sleep. We know, more or less, when we've had enough sleep. Yet a good night's sleep or a long afternoon nap may make us feel sleepier than we did before. We certainly know when we haven't had enough sleep; yet sleep deficits aren't easy to correct. It isn't possible just to bank sleep, so that we can withdraw what we need from our account.

Can we bank or store beauty? Even if we manage to hang onto what we've had rather than squander it, we still need to remain on the alert for more, since our hunger for beauty is constant. And yet given a glimpse, even if we recognize beauty, we aren't always sure what to do with it, where to put it. Those questions Hopkins poses are resonant because they have no easy answers. Again, the questions: What is beauty good for? asks "To What Serves Mortal Beauty?" How to keep back beauty from vanishing away? asks The Leaden Echo. It is as if we don't know how to take care of a mysterious animal we've happened upon and brought home. Or maybe what we're suddenly in possession of is an unknown but delicious substance. What would be the proper container for it? How best to preserve it?

Poetry is one preservative. When I flip through a book of poems, I often find initially that "a glance / Master more may than gaze." Before shutting the little Penguin edition of Hopkins, I find myself pausing at "The Blessed Virgin Compared to the Air We Breathe," a poem I never would have known if George hadn't happened to tell me that he had set it (long before we met) for counter-tenor and recorder. I possess no score of this, nor do I know whether it was ever recorded. But the poem is well worth reading and rereading. Its rhymed trimeter couplets constrain Hopkins to use relatively simple language. And unusually direct, too, is his startling command to the reader to stop, pay attention, look:

> Again, look overhead
> How air is azurèd;
> O how! nay do but stand
> Where you can lift your hand
> Skywards: rich, rich it laps
> Round the four fingergaps.
> Yet such a sapphire-shot,
> Charged, steepèd sky will not
> Stain light. Yea, mark you this:
> It does no prejudice.
> The glass-blue days are those
> When every colour glows,
> Each shape and shadow shows.

I love those four fingergaps. Like a jaded traveler suddenly galvanized by an ardent guide, I am stopped in my tracks by the command "nay do but stand," a phrase which reminds me of "See, it does this," another gestural, didactic moment, from "Mortal Beauty."

The distinctively Hopkinsonian adjective "steeped," as in "charged, steepèd sky," could lead me on to the apocalyptic sonnet "Spelt from Sibyl's Leaves," a poem whose pallid, lowering, livid tones George somehow managed to match with his musical setting:

For èarth | her bèing has unbóund; her dápple is at énd, as—
Tray or aswarm, all throughther, in throngs; | self in self
    stéepèd and páshed—quíte
Disremembering, dismembering | all now. Heart, you round
    me right
With: Óur évening is óver us; óur night | whélms, whélms, ánd
    will énd us.

But I'll stop there, with the remarkable image in "Blessed Virgin" of the sky lapping "round the four fingergaps." We mortals have to shield our eyes; we scrutinize the blazing blue sky through our spread fingers, lest we be overwhelmed by the beauty of the world. But we are still encouraged to look up.

These days, when I visit George at 80th Street, I try to bring not only cookies or chocolate or grapes, but also a book of poems—poems that reward rereading.

"Do you remember this?" I ask. "It's by Gerard Manley Hopkins. You set a lot of Hopkins. You never set this poem, but it's beautiful. Listen."

I read the poem to him. Sometimes he nods or smiles. Sometimes my voice breaks. Sometimes he falls asleep. And then, sometimes, I lie down next to him and sleep a little too.

THE SHADOWY SHORE

The first year you and I went up to the house in Vermont together, no sooner had we arrived than you sneezed and sneezed and sneezed. It was the middle of July; no doubt you were allergic to something. You took a pill you thought was an antihistamine, but it was really one of my sleeping pills (I was still a bad sleeper in those days). There were some of each in the bottle; I'd mixed them together. What on earth had I been thinking?

We'd taken the train up from New York to Montpelier Junction and hadn't slept much. So that summer morning on your first day in Vermont you fell asleep in the tub in the little bathroom in the attic, sun slanting in through the small window. Seeing you sprawled and snoring in the water, your knees bent so the claw-footed bathtub could accommodate your long body, I felt like Clytemnestra to your Agamemnon. Absurd analogy; I hadn't meant to harm you. Yet who else was at fault? It was, had I known it at the time, an ominous beginning to our visit; to our life together.

Somehow I helped you climb out of the tub, and you staggered to the bedroom and got into bed and slept for the next twelve hours or more. There was no reason to wake you even if I'd been able to. Some sleepers are hard to wake up. For example, as I was to learn during our son's early weeks some seven years after that unsettling morning in Vermont, it isn't easy to rouse a sleeping baby. Jonathan didn't want to nurse nearly as much as he wanted to sleep; simply to have been born was evidently exhausting.

When I visit you these days, you are often asleep. "Let him sleep," said the aide one afternoon not long ago, and I tucked your sock monkey between your chin and shoulder and pulled the American flag blanket over you and kissed you. Your suitemate Bill (the two of you share a bathroom neither of you can independently use) had recently been put on hospice care. Through the open door I peeked into his room as I left. He was fast asleep.

> The newborn emerging from gates and the dying
>   emerging from gates.
> The far advanced are to go on in their turns, and the far
>   behind are to go on in their turns. [1]

In the world I have gradually come to inhabit, a world abrim with sleep, I find myself thinking back to our nights in parallel: all those years of nights before you began to edge into the shadows; those fewer years, but plentiful enough, after you had begun to arrive there, and then the three or four years after you had largely disappeared into the darkness but we were still sharing a bed. Unlike the days once you woke up each morning, our nights

[1] All italicized quotes are from Whitman's "The Sleepers" (1855).

spent side by side felt, for quite a long time, habitual and comfortable and easy. You'd always been a much more proficient and copious sleeper than I, but with proximity and practice I had improved. Sleeping was something we could still do together; it was our last form of parallel play.

The time came, though, when I began to wish that you would not wake up so early, would not stride or stalk or stagger into another long and empty day. Every morning I'd get out of bed as quietly as I could, so as not to rouse you, but it almost never worked; before I knew it you'd be up and slithering into your clothes and out the door to buy a New York Times you could no longer read. I don't know exactly at what point I began to wish that you would not wake up at all, even if the price for that (did I consider this?) would be sleeping alone.

> It is I too... the sleepless widow looking out on the winter midnight.

But in so many ways I was a widow already.

Within the ramparts of sleep's cloudy castle, within the blurred parentheses of sleep, enfolded by sleep's heavy curtains, enshaded, as Keats says in his sonnet "To Sleep," in forgetfulness divine—from this drowsy vantage point, our times of wakefulness during the years before your illness begin now to look like an alien insert—lively enough, even exaggerated in their jumpiness, but of a wholly different substance from the thick stuff of sleep. To have been conscious together, to have been awake, has come to seem like the merest needle in the tall warm haystack where you and I slumbered. Plans, conversations, meals, sex, concerts, quarrels, even parenting: from the perspective of the present all these look small and frenetic as a puppet show. Meanwhile the backdrop of sleep looms ever larger and more convincing until it is no longer a backdrop but the scenery and stage and action simultaneously, the entire endless somnolent production in which we are involved.

We no longer live together. But even now, the continuity between our lives, the remaining ties that bind us, consist of sleep. You sleep in your bed in a small north-facing room on the second floor of a building on the East Side, and I sleep in our—in my—bed in a large south-facing room on the third floor of a building on the West Side. Sometimes I dream that you and I are talking together, and I think in the dream *There's nothing wrong after all, he's talking, he's fine*, and then I wake up. Sometimes you may dream about me or our son or the cats we've owned—the first pair, the second pair—or the summer mornings or the American Academy in Rome or the music you have written. But no one knows. Your dreams are locked inside you, and muteness has thrown away the key.

For over two years now I've been sleeping alone. As I begin to fill the empty space in the double bed, I still miss your warm presence, the light lattice-work of your long lithe body. And I find that I have stopped wishing for our parallel slumbers to end. At least most of the time, I am no longer impatient for your death.

It seems to me that everything in the light and air
      ought to be happy;
whoever is not in his coffin and the dark grave, let him know he
      has enough.

To roust you out of bed and put you out in the cold of death—would that be as arduous and cruel as waking someone deeply asleep, or would it be making no more than a minor adjustment to your current somnolent state? Either way, I no longer want—even if I were able— to interfere with your rest. When I visit you, when I think about you, you and I are floating down this murky stream together.

I turn but do not extricate myself
I would sound up the shadowy shore to which you are journeying.

Sometimes when I visit and find you asleep, instead of trying to wake you I lie down beside you.

I roll myself upon you as upon a bed . . . . resign myself to the
      dusk.

In this twilight where you and I spend so much time napping, we steer a drowsy course between death and sleep. Death: the suffering ends and everyone is finally equal. Sleep: the suffering is suspended and everyone is temporarily equal. Sleep and death both bring relief; it's easy to forget the difference, easy to confuse which of the two Whitman is referring to in his tender and heartbreaking evocation of the respite one or the other of them brings. It becomes easier and easier to feel that the distinction is so subtle as to be invisible.

> The consumptive, the erysipalite, he that is wronged, the antipodes, and every one between this and them in the dark, I swear they are averaged now . . . . one is no better than the other.
> The felon steps forth from the prison . . . . the insane becomes sane . . . . the suffering of sick persons is relieved,
> The sweatings and fevers stop . . . the throat that was unsound is sound.
> The lungs of the consumptive are resumed . . . . the poor distressed head is free.

Sooner or later, each visit ends. If we've been lying down, I get up and put the book or the half-corrected papers back into my bag and kiss you goodbye. I put on a CD of Mozart or Bach or Scarlatti or Schubert if none is on already. Sometimes you open your eyes; not often. I leave your room and punch the keypad by the door, open the door, and walk down the flight of stairs to the lobby. Then it's a short walk past the receptionist's desk to the front door, and I find myself once again on the leafy street. It's a quiet street, but still (and it's always a bit of adjustment) the city I have reentered is awake. This visit is over, but I'll be back.

> I stay awhile away O night, but I return to you again and love you. Why should I be afraid to trust myself to you?

Upstairs in your room, you sigh and stir on your bed, and go on voyaging into the dark.

PINDAR

Pindar wrote in his first Olympian Ode "best of all things is water." He was thinking of thirsty athletes rather than the shower at the Schervier Nursing Care Center in Riverdale. Nevertheless, there was something strikingly Pindaric—erotic, strenuous, torqued, baroque—in the elaborate process of getting my husband George into the shower. This undertaking was nothing if not an agon—a contest, a monumental struggle. Also, more Ovidian than Pindaric but entirely mythical, there was an element of metamorphosis involved. Was George a hero, a man, a boy, an infant, a centaur, or a stallion? Something of all these. There were the rolling eye, the raised hoof poised to kick. There was the diapered dumbness; there were the helplessness and fear and the abundant physical energy with its attendant threat. Abetted by aphasia, there was abundant confusion. His thoughts could not be known except through his body language, which itself was at this stage changing and chaotic, and his wishes were far from clear. Elaine the aide and I didn't know whether he knew who we were. We did know that he didn't want to take a shower.

One afternoon, a week or two after George had been

moved to Schervier, I was visiting. We were in his room, he stretched out on his bed, I in the single chair, probably with the television on or listening to music, when Elaine knocked on the door and peeked in. She wanted to know whether, since I was there, I'd be willing to try to help her get him into the shower. The bathroom was only a few steps from George's room. Did we undress him and get him into his bathrobe before proceeding to that white room? I think so, but I can't remember exactly, although I do clearly remember the mustard-colored terry-cloth bathrobe I'd bought at a thrift store. I also remember a pair of royal blue swimming trunks, and that I put these on him preparatory to the ablutions. I joked to Elaine that I hadn't brought my bathing suit this time, though I did bring it on the second attempt, since helping George to shower meant getting soaked.

If my husband was part hero, part horse, part man, and part infant, the process of getting him under the water was part hug, part dance, and part wrestling match, if you imagine each of these activities as involving not two people but three. Elaine and he and I were all working hard, using many of our muscles and (she and I) all our powers of persuasion and ingenuity. George was tall and strong and fast and slippery when wet.

That shower was one of the successful attempts, perhaps the only one. Once we three were in the shower room, I approached George, talking all the while as he stood there stripped and alert, bewildered and wary. Elaine was talking too. What were we saying to encourage him? I have no idea. Cajolery, persuasion, plea, praise—

all these, no doubt, as a sort of background music to the drama. "There, there, good boy," Elaine crooned. What I remember best of my role in this triangular activity isn't the probably meaningless words I said but the way I marshaled whatever resources I could. In addition to washcloth and soap, I was equipped with something Elaine lacked: George's and my shared past.

It wasn't only his slippery skin that I was hugging as we edged in a sort of lock-step toward the stream of warm water. It was every ounce and inch and moment I could muster of whatever trust and familiarity we had ever shared: each hour and minute, each month and year of a tranquillity that was now in the past. I knew perfectly well that that peaceful time was never going to come back; but I also knew that it was there somewhere, even if only in my memory (who knew what George remembered?), if I could only reach it. Somehow, it seemed to me that however remote they now seemed in the cruel light of his disease, those happy times were still available somewhere.

Memory isn't quite the right word. I tried to summon up in my body each grain and pore of those leisurely summer afternoons in Vermont when, sitting in his rocker on the porch, he'd smoke his pipe and blow smoke rings—or sometimes, to our small son's delight, blow bubbles filled with smoke. He'd stroll out to the end of the vegetable garden to stir the compost heap, or go upstairs to pace back and forth between his desk and the rickety old upright piano on the upstairs landing. He would try a phrase out again and again and set it down. All this was the kind of knowledge I was trying to instill into my arms and hands as I held and guided him, trying to coerce and reassure at once. In order to make this shower possible, my task as bath attendant was to help Elaine. But in order to do that, I first had to summon all these past times back; and to bring them back I had not only to remember them but also to believe that what had taken place in that suspiciously golden-looking age had been real. In Keats's phrase, I had to prove it on my pulses.

I took my courage up in my two hands and stood on tiptoe next to George under the warm water, my not quite five-foot seven to his not quite six-foot four, stretching up so that I could reach to shampoo his hair, which was soft and brown with hardly any grey. He raised his hands and helped to rub the lather in. And when he was rinsed and clean—we'd managed to soap his arms and legs and back and crotch—he knew, handed a clean towel, to reach up and dry his own wet hair. Triumph! Elaine, who had been standing on the other side of him during this whole process, hugged him, and he hugged her back.

Heracles diverting a river from its course to sluice out the Augean stables; Clytemnestra waiting by the tub with the bath sheet which will double as entangling net and shroud; the Danaids whose pitchers always leak—I am not any of these mythical figures, it is not the same situation, and yet in the charged and strenuous atmosphere of this, yes, heroic effort, I can't help sensing their presences all around me. Helen Keller is here too, holding her hands under a stream of water as Teacher pumps. The little girl is remembering the word she learned as a toddler before scarlet fever shut down her sight and hearing: wa-wa. Water. For Helen Keller, "water" will unlock the realm of language. For my husband, the key has long been lost, and it will not be found.

Best of all things is water, Pindar wrote. On a rare good day (there were not to be many more), a shower. One sunny June. One afternoon. One hour.

Q & A

I.

Although our daily lives are made up, to a great extent, of questions and answers, we mostly tend not to pay much attention to the Q and A format. It's as if the very pervasiveness of questions, their ubiquity, makes them transparent. True, the perennial flap over things like standardized testing—the weight of test scores, teaching to the test, and so on—may ultimately be seen under the rubric of questions and answers. But in the culture at large most questions and answers announce themselves more obviously in fixed routines. In game shows, for example, answers must be in the interrogative: a question is an answer and vice versa, and the whole enterprise is kept going by prize money. *Jeopardy*, the show I'm most familiar with, is a mild example. Another popular genre, advice columns, is also built around the twin pillars of the question and the answer. *Cris de coeur* are allowed, even expected, but confessions and outbursts must be couched in, or promptly lead to, the interrogative mood.

Questions and answers are hardly confined to conventional generic frameworks; they loom large in the routine but unpredictable interchanges that crop up many times a day, whenever we engage in conversation with someone else. Steven Pinker observes in *The Language Instinct* that

> language is so tightly woven into human experience that it is scarcely possible to imagine life without it. Chances are that if you find two or more people together anywhere on earth, they will soon be exchanging words.

Pinker doesn't need to add that the words they exchange will include questions and answers.

But if questions and answers are universal and often conventional, they may also be frustrating, elusive, and uneconomical. How rarely, for example, questions to which we really (*do you love me?*) or even mildly (*how do I look?*) crave an answer get replies at all. Yet wads, scads, gobs, reams of information surround us, or get hurled at us, constantly, in the form of answers to questions that we never asked at all or that we did ask but that we never expected, let alone wanted, to be answered. I am not referring here to the cataracts of information flooding in, or poised to flood in, from the electronic media. Human conversation presents us with more than enough.

Questions and answers often catch well-meaning speakers in a double bind. If I neglected to ask a question in the first place, out of a failure to intuit that a question needed to be inserted exactly here, then I bumblingly missed a social cue; I may appear churlish or self-centered. If, on the other hand, I did ask a question to which I innocently assumed no answer would be forthcoming because none was needed, and then found myself presented with a lengthy response, then perhaps someone else missed his or her social cue. Yet it often happens that no one fumbles the conversational ball. The game can become tedious, though: the problem is that unwritten social rules apparently require that we ask questions no matter how indifferent we are to the answers.

To scramble the signals further, we are also—as professionals, as parents, as customers, as clients, as neighbors—constantly put in the position of asking all kinds of questions to which we actually do want or need an answer. *Where does it hurt? How much does that cost? How do you get to X's house? Where were you last night?* Plenty of other questions, though, lack this kind of urgency. Although not one hundred percent specious, questions like *How's your mother doing? Are you having a nice vacation? How is your son/daughter liking college?* are nevertheless often closer to being formal gestures than they are to being genuine expressions of curiosity.

If only there were some simpler or more abstract way of signaling good will than concocting a question to the answer to which one is—at least I am—almost indifferent! For although there are exceptions, the range of my indifference expands over time. What fails to keep pace with this creeping dry patch is any sense of assurance that it's all right not to ask questions if I don't feel like it, and all right to ignore questions I don't want to answer. It is not all right; it's rude. Furthermore, more and more people out there seem to love asking questions. Many people even seem to love answering them.

But as should be clear by now, I am not a happy answerer. Of course all this rumination about questions and answers is connected with the fact that I've been having trouble lately even with questions that evidently need or deserve answers. The waitress, the hairdresser, even my sister off to the grocery store to do an errand—all have legitimate and reasonable questions to which I should surely know the answers. Which kind of jam do I prefer? Do I usually blow dry my hair? What kind of toothpaste do I want her to get?

And yet I feel like Andy Osnard in *The Tailor of Panama*, who can't or won't answer the discreet sartorial query as to whether he dresses on the right or the left, replying instead "Damned if I know; it flops about like a windsock." These endless practical questions are perfectly normal, but they are also profoundly boring, and something more: they seem to presume that the questionee knows and cares about every petty detail. I remember saying as much (less biliously, I hope) to Alison Lurie when she kindly gave me dinner in Key West. She asked all the guests what kind of tea—mint, ginger, Earl Grey, and so on—we wanted with our key lime pie, and I made some comment about the embarrassment of riches on offer. Alison said, though I can't remember her exact words, that people have so little choice in the larger matters of their lives that it is a kindness to offer them a choice of (say) teas—not a thought I found reassuring.

Do I then want never to have my preference consulted? Maybe only on larger matters. I want to be asked important questions—at least middlingly important—and to let the details take care of themselves. Or maybe what I want is to be asked, or given answers to, questions I never thought of asking.

II.

Problematic questions have a venerable history. *Am I my brother's keeper? Where wast thou when I laid the foundations of the earth?* To Socrates and Jesus, two great teachers who famously preferred talking in place of writing, it came naturally to deal in the interrogative. Socrates, an incorrigible poser of questions, rarely answered them to his own or anyone else's satisfaction—as Euthyphro says, the answers seem to walk away. Jesus's teachings generated questions to which his recorded answers (*render unto Caesar* is probably the best example) are so apt and pungent that the disciples, and the multitudes, and even the interrogating Satan, who occasion these replies can seem like so many straight men.

Closer to us in time is Thoreau. Although, as Stanley Cavell has pointed out, this writer habitually uses "neighbor" as a synonym for "fellow human being," he also tells us "I love to be alone." Certainly Thoreau gives the impression of preferring his own company to that of human visitors with their predictable and persistent questions. Indeed, before the first paragraph of *Walden* has reached its conclusion, Thoreau has launched into an explanation which seems to be part justification for the book he has just written and part something more resembling a complaint, albeit a characteristically hedged and ambiguous complaint:

> I should not obtrude my affairs so much on the notice of my readers if very particular inquiries had not been made by my townsmen concerning my mode of life, which some would call impertinent, though they do not appear to me at all impertinent, but, considering the circumstances, very natural and pertinent.

Cavell notes that the clause "which some would call impertinent" points in two directions: is it the inquiries which are impertinent, or is it Thoreau's "mode of life"? True, Thoreau swiftly clears up the momentary ambiguity, but not before managing to implant the suggestion that one way to read the book that will follow is to consider it an answer to countless repetitive questions—questions which may be considered impertinent because they're irrelevant, or simply because they're rude.

He then continues:

> Some have asked what I got to eat; if I did not feel lonesome; if I was not afraid; and the like. Others have been curious to learn what portion of my income I devoted to charitable purposes; and some, who have large families, how many poor children I maintained. I will therefore ask those of my readers who feel no particular interest in me to pardon me if I undertake to answer some of these questions in this book.

Is Thoreau here implying that the curious neighbors are responsible for the existence of his book—that he finally sat down and wrote *Walden* to answer their questions once and for all? His style and thought are too edgy and feline for this to seem a complete answer. That determination to confront intrusive questions is, however, what one gets in a book by a later writer working in Thoreau's tradition.

We Took to the Woods by Louise Dickinson Rich (interestingly, a descendant of Emily Dickinson), published in 1942, is an account of the author's life in southwestern Maine, an area of the state that is remote even now. Rich approaches her friends' (the word she uses) apparently insatiable curiosity about her life in the woods in a far more straightforward and friendly manner than Thoreau. She puts the friends' queries to work, naming each of her eleven chapters after a frequently asked question and then using the chapter to address the question: "But How Do You Make a Living?"; "Why Don't You Write a Book?"; and so on. So far as I recall, Rich never mentions Thoreau, but his presence can be felt in various ways in her chapter headings and elsewhere; the question about making a living, for example, corresponds to Thoreau's opening chapter, "Economy."

Rich is a lively and sympathetic writer whose book I have long enjoyed, but she is no Thoreau; and long before one has finished *We Took to the Woods*, the relation of each question to its eponymous chapter has become increasingly and annoyingly predictable. Though Rich would not, of course, have countenanced or even understood this terminology, she could be said to use each chapter to "deconstruct" the questions it purports to answer. *Of course* living in the woods is worthwhile; no, she doesn't get lonely in any way that matters (she does have a husband and child, by the way); and so on. Rich is far more gracious and indulgent, not to mention hospitable, to her offstage chorus of ever-curious and insistently conventional unnamed friends than Thoreau would ever be. Yet unless I'm projecting, I sometimes sense, particularly in more recent revisitings of Rich's book, that she is growing as impatient with them as the Maine guides are with "sports," ignorant city slickers. Sometimes I even wonder whether these "friends" are fictive, mere occasions for expatiating on her rural life, as Thoreau's "townsmen" also sometimes seem to be.

III.

If we turn from prose to poetry, the problematic nature of the interlocutor—the questioner, the visitor, the friend— seems to vanish. The dynamic is altogether different: poems ask questions without always expecting answers; they regularly answer questions no one has necessarily asked; and all this without intrusiveness, impertinence, embarrassment. Indeed, although I didn't use to be as allergic to questions as I've recently become, I find myself wondering whether my love of poetry hasn't always been connected to the way poems combine intimacy and tact.

One reason poems aren't impertinent is that they can't help pertaining to something. Whatever their formal allegiances, poems inhabit a kind of protected space where utterance both does and does not take place out loud; where a question or a remark both does and profoundly does not expect an answer. Poetry's relation to the quotidian world, the place where people want to know which side you dress on and whether you prefer blue cheese or Italian dressing on your salad, corresponds to the relation of the classroom to the "real world": more shaped by convention and hence in a way safer, shielding its denizens with a code of conduct. Having said this, of course, I concede that the salad dressing questions are in their own way also conventional, and many people are no doubt as bored by the questions asked by poetry as I am by questions about petty preferences. Perhaps the call and response of jazz, or the questions and answers of liturgy, are other ways of taking the deadly ennui out of our daily dealings in the interrogative mood by making them opportunities for performance.

In any case, poetry is intent on having its cake and eating it too. When poetry deals with questions, as it often does, no one loses, everyone gains. One way to look at poetry, in fact, is to think of it as a motherlode of unanswered, dangling questions and at the same time of spontaneous, unprovoked answers. If that description makes the entire genre of lyric sound like a Bedlam where some inmates huddle in corners mumbling to themselves while others declaim rhetorically to thin air, so be it.

Poetry embraces a wide range of temperaments and

behaviors: lonely, impulsive, cooperative, histrionic, isolated, self-sufficient, aggressive, confiding. Some poems resemble wallflowers (flower in the crannied wall, wrote Tennyson), refusing to open up; some are more like shy students whose questions go unanswered because they aren't audible in the front of the room; some are like strangers who suddenly turn to you and confide their secrets. Or one could turn this formulation around and say that any one of these socially challenged personality types is behaving like some kind of poem.

Poems ask all kinds of questions. Some are urgently in need of answers:

> What men or gods are these?

> Who are these coming to the sacrifice?

But whatever their hunger for a reply, poems never just stand there waiting. They do something more interesting; rather than demand an answer from us, the poem transmits the question to us and so it becomes our question.

> To be or not to be, that is the question.

Poems also ask questions which go unanswered because they are unanswerable questions, to which no adequate reply can really be expected.

> What immortal hand or eye
> Dare frame thy fearful symmetry?

is a famous example. Like Keats's questions in Ode to a Grecian Urn, Blake's questions in "The Tyger" crescendo to a climax, the original question breaking up into a number of slightly breathless shorter questions—none of which is answered. Poetic questions can do without answers; what they must have is pace, poise, authority.

> Ô saisons, Ô chateaux,
> Quelle âme est sans défauts?

> How with this rage shall beauty hold a plea,
> Whose action is no stronger than a flower?

> Who made the eyes but I?

> Where are the snows of yesteryear?

> In silks that whistled, who but he?

> Tis de bios, ti de terpnon ater chryses Aphrodites?

To call such questions rhetorical may be technically correct, but it doesn't capture the potential range of rhetoric. There is surely a difference, however subtle, between asking a question for effect without expecting an answer and asking a question which seems to thirst intensely for an answer despite the essential recognition that it will not and cannot be answered. Questions in poems often have that latter dimension—a wry, wistful longing.

I mentioned pace and poise. Often poems containing questions do not begin abruptly with the question; rather, they rise to its occasion. Again the analogy here is with the classroom situation rather than real life. Good poems manage to embed their questions in the ongoing pattern or flow of discourse, rather than baldly posing them.

> I wonder, by my troth, what thou and I
> Did, till we loved? Were we not wean'd till then,
> But sucked on country pleasures, childishly?

Some poems, of course, do begin with questions; in that case, before the poem ends, the question needs to be opened up and transformed into something else: an assertion, a refrain, an exhortation.

> Being your slave, what should I do but tend
> Upon the hours and times of your desire?

It is the rare poem that succeeds in ending with a question. In another pleasingly unlifelike development, questions embedded in poems quite often do provide their own answers. Sometimes, delightfully, the answers come after a pause during which something else is going on.

> Cui dono lepidum novum libellum,
> arido modo pumicum expolitum?
> Corneli, tibi...

> Then from our gnarled (his name?)
> Boatman (Gennaro!) burst
> Some local, vocal gem
> Ten times a day rehearsed.

Sometimes, without much in the way of a pause, the poem answers its own question, but in another voice:

Mistress Mary quite contrary, how does your garden grow?
With silver bells and cockle shells and pretty maids all in a row.

> Tell me where is fancy bred,
> Or in the heart, or in the head?
> How begot, how nourished?
> Reply, reply.
> It is engend'red in the eyes,
> With gazing fed, and fancy dies
> In the cradle where it lies.

The other side of the interrogative coin is the answer, whether unexpected or expected. Just as poems often ask questions which go unanswered, they sometimes answer questions no one has asked. Suddenly, startlingly, poems can confide in us, telling us out of the blue something we hadn't known we needed to hear while simultaneously and invisibly creating a need in us to hear it. The need is crucial; poems which fail to command or hold our attention have not managed to generate an appetite in us for what they are saying—a problem which is all too reminiscent of the buttonholing bores one encounters in real life. Life and poetry meet in the arena of embarrassment when Wordsworth in "Resolution and Independence" depicts—as Lewis Carroll in "A-Sitting on a Gate" hilariously parodies—the social awkwardness of asking a sincere question to whose answer the speaker is then too abstracted to pay attention. A nice touch of Carroll's parody is that the old man repeatedly asks for a little cash tip, though the speaker predictably and repeatedly fails to take the hint. I confess that I, too, when persistently questioned, have sometimes been tempted to ask for a small reimbursement.

Paying attention to what is said to you, making sure people are listening before you launch into a story—these are matters of manners in our lives. That literature too—not poetry alone—can have good or bad manners is a point charmingly discussed by James Merrill in both a 1967 interview with Donald Sheehan and a 1972 interview with David Kalstone. Without particularly focusing on the matter of questions, though he touches on this when citing Stephen Crane, Merrill connects the writer's verbal choices (tense; person) with the atmosphere—inviting or otherwise—the literary work offers:

> Maybe there's something worth saying about tenses here, about how one handles them. Last winter I visited a workshop in which only one out of fifteen poets had noticed that he needn't invariably use the first-person present active indicative. Poem after poem began: "I empty my glass . . . I go out . . . I stop by woods. . . ." For me a "hot" tense like that can't be handled for very long without cool pasts and futures to temper it; or some complexity of syntax, or a modulation into the conditional—some alternative relation to experience. Otherwise, you get this addictive, self-centered immediacy, harder to break oneself of than cigarettes. That kind of talk (which, by the way, is purely literary; it's never heard in life unless from foreigners or four-year-olds) calls to mind a speaker suspicious of words, in great boots, chain-smoking, Getting It Down on Paper. He'll never notice "Whose woods these are I think I know"

gliding backwards through the room, or "Longtemps je me suis couché de bonne heure" plumping a cushion invitingly at her side. . . .

In the Sheehan interview, Merrill comments:

It's hard to imagine a work of literature that doesn't depend on manners, at least negatively. One of the points of a poem like Ginsberg's *Howl* is that it uses an impatience with manners very brilliantly; but if there had been no touchstone to strike that flint upon, where would Ginsberg be?

And manners—whether good or bad—are entirely allied with tone or voice in poetry. If the manners are inferior, the poem will seem unreal or allegorical as in some of Stephen Crane's little poems. Take the one in which the man is eating his heart and the stranger comes up and asks if it's good. Those are bad manners for a stranger. Consequently the poem ends shortly after it begins because they have nothing more to say to each other. On the other hand, a poem like George Herbert's "Love" goes on for three stanzas; in a situation fully as "unreal" as Crane's, two characters are being ravishingly polite to one another.

Good manners in poems nearly always represent a triumph of artistry over the narcissistic thirst of the actual person who wrote the poem—a person who is more than likely to feel, often with a degree of truth, that she or he is being unjustly neglected. Every week I get letters from fellow poets who wisely siphon off their feelings of isolation in letters instead of letting them leak into their poems. The letters, accordingly, tend to contain a measure of self-pity; but letters are a better place for this. Two recent examples, both from letters which were accompanied by new poems:

> A) I must admit I had a hard time for a while dealing with the deafening silence that has so far greeted my collected poems, although I've worked it out and feel okay now. (Noise was not the reason for writing all those poems in the first place.)
> B) I love writing, but it is without doubt a lonely business.

The poems enclosed in these letters had nothing to do with self-pity or solipsism.

IV.

Outside the rarefied and relatively humane realm of poetry, in the higgledy-piggledy of human interchange, we—women, men, parents, children, teachers, students, family, friends—manage as best we can. My good friend E and I walk almost daily in Riverside Park. A natural question-asker both from genuine curiosity and by upbringing—that is, one whom nature and nurture have conspired to push toward interrogation—E has nevertheless learned over the years not to ask me too many questions. If she does, I bristle. In fact she no longer needs to ask me many, nor I to ask her; each of us is sufficiently up to date with the goings on in the other's life that we needn't prod for more details. The questions we ask come from familiarity, not obligation, and anyway quite early on in our walks they tend to give way to overlapping women's talk; the awkward staccato rhythm of Q and A has become fluent, elided.

If as a friend I have sometimes been vexed by being asked too many questions, in my experience as a mother the shoe has been on the other foot, or the foot has been in the maternal mouth. By the time he was ten, my son already disliked being asked questions (at least questions asked by me) much more markedly than I do now. Without any specific injunction on his part that I can recall, indeed probably without his having said a word, I inferred that we should work out a compromise. When we walked home together from his school, I could use the time to ask him three questions each day. If I was silly enough to squander the twenty minutes on inquiries like "What did you have for lunch today?" or "Do you have lots of homework tonight?" or (worse still) "How was school?" I was putting myself in the position of the foolish fisherman in the fairy tale who gets and promptly wastes three wishes. As in a fairy tale, too, I would sometimes feel that toads or black puddings were plopping out of my mouth whenever I opened it. I think also of Papageno's padlocked lips, though Papageno's particular vice was chattering, not asking questions.

The three-question rule didn't mean I was ever required to ask my son anything at all. Would it therefore be legitimate to hoard unasked questions and add them to my permissible quota the next afternoon? I never tried this, and I seriously doubt that I would have been allowed to get away with it.

Like many academics, including plenty of other people in my family, my father was a professional question-asker. A renowned teacher, he also reportedly enjoyed asking certain students questions they must have found mortifying as well as unanswerable: "So tell me, Father O'Reilly, what do you think of these Homeric gods who fuck mortal women?" Could he really have asked a hapless graduate student this question in the fifties? Tradition hasn't preserved the student's answer, if there was any.

But I am more interested here in the obscure area of my mother's questions and answers. As a mother, I know that not all of one's questions to one's children are answered—if not when the children are small, then certainly not when they are teenagers. On the other hand, it is rare for children to ask their mothers questions, at least certain kinds of questions: are you tired, would you like another helping, an extra blanket, how late will you be out? Such questions belong to the mother's script, not the child's. When Cedric in *Little Lord Fauntleroy* calls his mother "Dearest," the effect is as wince-making as if he had commanded her to clean her plate.

Maybe my son's economy with words derives from his maternal grandmother as well as from his father (clearly, he doesn't get it from me), for my own mother was hardly loquacious. The opposite of a poet who answers questions that haven't been asked, my mother neither answered unspoken questions nor asked unnecessary ones. When, however, questions were asked that demanded an answer, she was terse but judicious.

Lately I have been remembering two of my mother's

answers to questions I asked her when I was a child, questions whose answers (which may well be why they stand out in my mind) were in their very different ways not easy for her to utter. I asked other questions that carried no emotional baggage—what was a dictator? why did figures in modern paintings look distorted? are two I still recall—to which I received informative answers. But the two questions I am thinking of now were more problematic.

Both of them arose from my overhearing my mother's half of a telephone conversation. The first call, it was easy to infer, was some invitation or other which my mother refused on the grounds that she and my father would be busy on the evening in question—an evening when I must have known she would in fact be free.

"Why did you say you were going to be busy on Friday, Mommy?" I asked, or words to that effect.

She hesitated for a beat and then answered, with a grave emphasis which was somehow an implicit acknowledgment of the world's complexity, "Honey, it was a social lie." And then she went on, I guess, to explain what she had just demonstrated—exactly what a social lie was for and how it worked.

The other call, when I was a bit older, was of a different order of magnitude. I don't know who the person at the other end of the line was; most likely it was my mother's brother-in-law, because something serious was evidently being said that concerned Aunt Mary, my mother's sister. As soon as my mother was off the phone (and I don't remember the expression on her face), I was quick with my question.

"Mommy, what happened to Aunt Mary?"

Again that slight pause. And also, I seem to remember, something more—something in the silence, or in her facial muscles, or the bend of her head—which indicated a stiffening of resolve. It was not a clenching of what Homer calls the gates of the teeth; on the contrary, she was summoning strength, steeling herself to convey accurately what needed to be communicated. There was no question of euphemism or evasion.

"She hanged herself," answered my mother.

Four syllables, three words. These sufficed for me to understand what didn't need to be said: that not only was her elder sister's suicide a hard thing, but being its messenger was hard too. Hard in part, I speculated much later, because the two sisters had not got on very well for many years; hence some of my mother's grief may have sprung from her lack of grief, which is not the same as lack of feeling. My aunt left her husband and five children, of whom the youngest was only thirteen.

What was my reaction at the time? I don't remember whether I tried to comfort her; I doubt that I questioned her further. Things had to be done, but—her three words implied—there was little more to say.

Around the same time I had begun to remember my honest, laconic mother's handling of these questions, I was visited by a vivid dream—one of those rare and precious dreams in which our beloved dead are matter-of-factly restored to life in a recognizable form, without too much distortion or static. In the dream, I and my mother—she seemed to be about the age I am now—were in a bedroom (my old bedroom?) in our apartment on Riverside Drive. In addition, she was on the phone (there was never a telephone in that room); I knew without being told that at the other end of the line was Jason Epstein, who was calling to invite her out to lunch at Le Cirque.

Jason Epstein, I should note, had been one of my father's students at Columbia in the 1950s. At the most recent of my rare encounters with him, some time earlier this year, he had exclaimed on how much I looked like my mother, and then (perhaps a bit confusingly for the others present) immediately dredged up a recollection of me at the age of two or three "climbing over the back of a chair." At the latter moment in this foreshortened temporal scheme, I had presumably resembled my mother less.

Back in the dream: my mother had evidently accepted Jason's invitation, and deciding what to wear to such a swanky restaurant was a challenge for her. So she and I went through a closetful of droopy, stained, or otherwise shabby outfits. (Recently, in my waking life, I'd read a peppy magazine article about discarding all non-essentials from one's closet.) But more salient than the matter of wardrobe was the conversation she and I had while we were going through the clothes (her clothes? mine? shared?).

From overhearing my mother's half of the phone conversation with Jason, I had gathered that as old friends do, he had asked her for some accounting of her life. (Her life since he had last seen her? Her life up until, or perhaps since, her death?).

"What did he want you to tell him about your life, Mom?" Just as in my childhood, so in the dream: once she was off the phone I peppered her with questions.

Her answer was Janus-faced—a dream answer. "He told me," she said, "to begin the story from the beginning and just go on." But she also seems to me to have answered: "He told me to start in the present and work my way backward."

Whatever the command had been, I had overheard my mother trying over the phone to oblige Jason, who even in the dream was clearly his authoritative self. However she had chosen to relate the story of her life, she said of the task, once off the phone, "It wasn't easy." What wasn't easy? Telling him her story. But what story exactly? Here is where the reported narrative within the dream goes blurry. The only fragment that stays with me is that she reported to me that she told Jason "I did it twice."

This answer only raised more questions. Did what twice? When I thought about this characteristically terse fragment later, I thought of her having given birth twice, having raised two daughters. This interpretation neatly— too neatly—whisks the focus off my mother and onto my sister and me, in a way entirely typical of a child's smug perception of her centrality in her mother's life— also, perhaps, in keeping with my mother's self-effacing temperament.

But on second thought, peeling the dream layers back, I think that my mother's "twice" referred to more than maternity. Maybe—although this is another self-centered interpretation—my mother's saying she had "done it twice" was my dream-coded reference to the childhood memories of the two answers she had given to my questions.

One: *Honey, it was a social lie.* Two: *She hanged herself.* As if these two stark sentences were all the tools my mother had given me before she left me to the business of figuring life out on my own.

How far does that pair of answers take me? This far: that all answers since those two—not easy, it wasn't easy, as she told me—are by comparison wordy and evasive. What does it mean that I myself grew up to become a word-weaver, but one who has trouble with questions and answers, at least the questions other people ask me? Asking myself what the dream meant, that further question is as close as I come to an answer.

DREAMS

On Sunday morning, October 23, 2011, I awoke from a dream of a warm green lagoon through which I'd been struggling waist-deep. I'd floundered up sunken stairs and splashed through deserted arcades festooned with Spanish moss, all the while warily skirting monsters: fat sleepy marine creatures, torpid, half-submerged, but dangerous nevertheless.

The dream felt familiar, almost like one of a series; I seemed to have been dreaming versions of it for months. There was always the same arduous quest and/or flight, the same hedged relief at waking unscathed from one more fearful labor in a series that seemed endless. Except there had been no monsters until now. Avalanches, hurricanes, mountain peaks, blizzards, black rivers trickling toward the underworld: yes. But reptiles with jaws open to devour me were something new.

The day went on. That morning, a long and long-planned phone conversation with a colleague about the poetry students I was to inherit from her in the spring semester. At noon, I was a guest at a wedding lunch in a midtown Italian restaurant: lots of food and an unaccustomed amount of mid-day wine. Back home, I dropped in at about five o'clock on my next-door neighbor Jill's shiva for her father, who had suddenly died earlier in the week while she and he were celebrating his new teaching job (he was seventy) with a trip to India. Stunned with shock and jetlag, Jill was surrounded by friends; her husband and two young sons were there, and there were piles of food and more wine. Tears, laughter, hugs.

Wedding and shiva: these rites of passage, and all the food and wine, were conducive to an early evening nap, from which I woke up more or less refreshed. I took a bath, I remember, and put on my new leopard-spotted leggings and puttered around getting ready for the week to come. I watched the ten o'clock news while simultaneously brushing one of my cats (a cozy ritual for us both), and hadn't yet gotten myself into bed when, at 10:45, the call came from the nursing home where my husband had been installed earlier in the month. George, who had been ill with dementia for years, and whose increasingly frequent and severe crises had surely occasioned my dreams of frantic quest and peril, had recently taken a turn for the worse. The call informed me that he had died.

\#

In however skewed and subterranean and unproveable a fashion, dreams—in my experience, and not only in mine—seem central to tracing, even if never wholly comprehending, the patterns of experience. It is as if we understand dreams even when we don't remember them. In this dreams are the opposite of stories, even though stories are surely composed of dream-stuff, and even though when we tell our dreams we have to use shreds and threads drawn from the web of story.

Or else we remember dreams even when we don't understand them. In this, too, dreams are the opposite of stories, even though when we tell dreams we tell them in the guise of stories, and when we tell a story we are nailing narrative scaffolding to the cloudy substance of dreams.

Sleep's book holds more than we can ever read. We stick a finger in the text, pull out a plum and taste it, lick our finger. Later, in the middle of the morning, a ghost taste floats back.

#

Thinking of all this, I was startled at the animus displayed by Michael Chabon in a recent review of *Finnegans Wake*. Granted that the sheer scale and difficulty of this novel might give any dream aficionado pause; but Chabon seems oddly bitter and draconian in his witty condemnation of dreams. Perhaps as befits a novelist, he seems especially irked by the narrative shortcomings dreams present. "The wisdom of dreams," he complains, "is a fortune on paper that you can't cash out, an oasis of shimmering water that turns, when you wake up, to a mouthful of sand. I hate [dreams] for their absurdities and deferrals, their endlessly broken promise to amount to something by and by. I hate them for the way they ransack memory, jumbling treasure and trash ... Pretty much the only thing I hate more than my dreams are yours....At the breakfast table in my house, an inflexible law compels all recountings of dreams to be compressed into a sentence or, better still, half a sentence, like the paraphrasing of epic films listed in *TV Guide*: 'Rogue samurai saves peasant village.'"

Chabon's grudge against dream narration recalls that of another novelist who, at least while wearing his critical hat, inveighs against dreams—this time, not dreams as brokenly recounted at breakfast but as used with (of all things) excessive efficiency by novelists. In *Aspects of the Novel*, E.M. Forster comments crossly that novelists' approach to sleep is "...perfunctory. No attempt to indicate oblivion or the actual dream world. Dreams are either logical or else mosaics made out of hard little fragments of the past and future. They are introduced with a purpose and that purpose is not the character's life as a whole, but that part of it he lives while awake. He is never conceived as a creature, a third of whose time is spent in darkness. It is the limited daylight vision of the historian, which the novelist elsewhere avoids. Why should he not understand or reconstruct sleep? For remember, he has the right to invent, and we know when he is inventing truly, because his passion floats us over improbabilities. Yet he has neither copied sleep nor created it. It is just an amalgam."

Forster protests too much. Two of the novelists of whom he writes admiringly elsewhere in *Aspects*, Proust and Dostoevsky, both make wonderful and not at all mechanistic use of dreams; in fact in his "Prophecy" chapter Forster cites Mitya's visionary dream in *The Brothers Karamazov*. Still, it may be that dreams are more at home in poetry than in fiction (a possibility entertained by neither Chabon nor Forster). Homer, Aeschylus, Shakespeare, Keats, Eliot, Machado, Bogan, Merrill, and a host of other poets have used dreams to stunning thematic effect. Granted, these dreams are often (in a way true to life) hard to interpret. Early in the *Iliad* a false dream visits Agamemnon; late in the *Odyssey*, Penelope asks the disguised Odysseus to help her interpret her dream about geese. For that matter, Stepan Arkadyevich, at the beginning of *Anna Karenina*, has trouble recalling the details of his jolly dream about tumblers.

The puzzling out of the elusive meanings of dreams has been a human occupation (even profession) for so long that it seems clear that not only dreams, but also our stubborn attempts to ferret out or pin down their meanings, are part of our human heritage. Dreams may, as Chabon grumbles, break "their promise to amount to something," but something that at least feels meaningful is often saved from the jumble. Whether in literature or in life, would we really want to do without dreams? "Dreams ransack memory," says Chabon, sounding like a policeman. In his luminous new book *On Poetry*, Glyn Maxwell expresses this idea more gently: "Dreams are memory-catchers."

#

Now that more than a year has passed since my husband's death, the complicated day he died looks different. The wedding and the shiva, food and wine, laughter and tears; perhaps these were the dream. The soupy green lagoon, the yawning monsters: were these not the world in which I'd lived, my difficult terrain through the long years of George's illness? Like the Ancient Mariner, I seem to want people to know my story, which is beginning to be mercifully indistinguishable from a dream which was frightening at the time but which one is beginning to forget. Even the monsters switch their tails and grin at me.

WOODLAWN

At nine in the morning on October 26, as arranged, I rendezvous with my guide, Lou Blumengarden, on the platform of the #4 subway to Woodlawn Cemetery in the Bronx. The ride to Woodlawn, at the end of the line, lasts perhaps twenty-five minutes. So from before ten in the morning till two in the afternoon, in Lou's knowledgeable and enthusiastic company (both these adjectives are feeble understatements), I explore the quiet boulevards of this 400-acre necropolis. We take plenty of detours. I sometimes plead fatigue, but "You have to see the most beautiful/ugliest/showiest example of carving, just over here," Lou will exhort, and off we go again. Having given tours of Woodlawn for some fifteen years, he knows what he's doing. Today, for better or worse, I have him all to myself, or vice versa.

I first met Lou a few winters ago, when we were both—as we still are—participants in the Walk on the Wild Side program offered by the American Museum of Natural History. These walks are an ingenious fund-raising device: support the Museum at a certain fairly modest level and you're eligible to roam the Museum's miles of corridor one morning a week, before the the place is open to the public, from January through March. While our group of anywhere from twenty to forty New Yorkers, mostly of a certain age, do our preliminary warmup stretches, a docent gives a short talk on Theodore Roosevelt, dinosaurs, frogs, global warming, or whatever the topic may be. Then, a thundering herd, we stride from eight to nine on various routes: through the light-flooded Planetarium, or the murky hall with the Pacific Indian totem poles, or around the canoe that Holden Caulfield enjoyed peeping into to see if he could glimpse the squaw's uncovered breasts. Then cool-down exercises, another short talk, and it's time for breakfast in a hall of African mammal dioramas—coffee and fruit and muffins and lots of chitchat, all under the abstracted gaze of gorillas or okapis.

Lou, who's retired from I can never remember what job (was he a civil servant?), is a docent at AMNH as well as a tour guide elsewhere in the city; he's coaxed several fellow Walkers on the Wild Side to tour Woodlawn with him, and this mild fall Friday was the day I could finally do it. What highlights stand out? There's the modest stone of Gertrude Ederle, who, I learn, swam the English Channel in 1926 at the age of eighteen and was honored by a ticker-tape parade. Her father, Lou informs me, ran a butcher shop on Amsterdam Avenue. There are many more illustrious names: Elizabeth Cady Stanton is here, and Miles Davis, and Admiral Farragut, and Fiorello LaGuardia, and too many others to name, as well as plenty of more obscure people.

Against a soft grey sky, the fall foliage is gold and orange. "Look at that cut-leaf maple!" crows Lou competitively. "You wouldn't see anything better than that in Vermont." Vermont: more trees, more massed color, fewer graves. More deer, fewer mausoleums. At lunchtime we adjourn to an Irish deli on Katonah Avenue (the place sells Irish tea, shortbread, canned goods, and newspapers) and then eat our wraps at a staff picnic table behind the cemetery's offices. After lunch we set out again; we haven't yet seen Melville's tomb, or Louis Sherry's, or Juilliard's. Lou wants to make sure to point out the Archipenko relief sculpture of the child I hadn't known Fiorello LaGuardia and his wife lost.

Melville's modestly sized monument features a haunting empty scroll, which both suggests unfinished work and seems to invite the passerby to incise his or her own thoughts. On top of the reddish granite gravestone, I'm happy to note, quite a few visitors have left pebbles.

Not far from where Melville lies, also memorable, is the tomb of the Arctic explorer Delong. Delong, who died, with his entire crew, on an expedition in 1881, seems to be stretching like a Rodin figure out of his jacket of stone. Wearing a hooded parka, he shades his eyes with his right hand against invisible but clearly blinding wind and snow.

At a recent reading at the Cornelia Street Cafe, the octogenarian poet Stanley Moss read a poem containing the lines "The dead are trees. / We are cut from their lumber." Other lines I jotted down, as if in preparation for today's tour: "Sooner or later / I hope you will lie on

my grey stone." Also: "How long from Is to Will Be to
Was? Not long." My friend Rowan Ricardo Phillips, a poet
almost fifty years Moss's junior, also read. Rowan's debut
collection is entitled *The Ground*; in a recent interview,
he called the ground "the street level of the imagination,
where heaven and hell declare themselves."

Here at street level (and Woodlawn, like any city,
is divided into streets and lanes and avenues), one's
imagination does indeed reach up and down. Where, for
example, do I want to end (end up, as it were)? Not—this
visit confirms the feeling—in a mausoleum, a hollow
house of stone. It seems at once sinister and reassuring
that the dead should have a little suburb to themselves. A
lonely suburb; Lou and I pass one funeral in progress, but
otherwise, except for the black squirrels dodging silently
among the tombs and a few groundsmen driving by in
trucks or chipping branches, we have the place pretty
much to ourselves.

How light a footprint would you leave, if it were
up to you? Lou seems irked by the mausolea (Pupin?
Juilliard?) that have grown shabby because no funds
were earmarked for their upkeep. All Juilliard's money,
he tells me, went to the Juilliard School—exactly (I think)
where it belongs. Lou prefers Woodlawn to Greenwood
Cemetery in Brooklyn because you get a higher class of
corpse in the former. "The 99% have no imagination" he
says. "The 1% make beautiful monuments for themselves,
and if I win the lottery, that's what I'll do."

One mausoleum I concur with Lou in admiring is that
of the Straus family. The memorial statue and fountain in

Straus Park, a few blocks from where I live, are beautiful; but the low building here, around three sides of a central courtyard, is restrained and eloquent. It's distinguished by an Egyptian-looking galley at the entrance, a death ship carved from some dark stone. The tomb atop which this black galley rests holds the remains, Lou tells me, only of Isidor. After the Titanic sank, Ida's body was never recovered.

I'm not surprised to learn that Woodlawn locks its gates at night. Halloween is approaching, but there will be no revelry or deviltry here, maybe only a quiet reunion of ghosts. As it happens, trick or treaters of every stripe, most of them adults judging by their height, are out in force the next night, when I take the subway down to Chambers Street. October 31 is still a few days away, but whether because this is a Saturday night or because everyone knows a hurricane is expected to reach the area on Monday, Halloween is evidently being celebrated tonight. Before my companion and I even board the downtown express, we see two six-foot penguins with big yellow feet. In the subway car are cowboys and cowgirls with matching pink bandannas. There are warriors and princesses and a general carnival spirit, and it's only eight o'clock.

We're on our way to another kind of ingenious fundraiser: the second annual Poetry Sleepover at Poets' House. The latest home of this organization is a sturdy glass structure near Battery Park City, perilously near the river but in the event unscathed by Hurricane Sandy. You pay a modest fee, not to walk museum corridors but to bring your sleeping bag, a toothbrush, a flashlight, and a notebook, and bed down between the bookshelves in Poets' House's library. (Poets' House was founded by Stanley Kunitz and others who had sensibly realized that poets tend to have libraries of poetry to bequeath.)

Kristin Prevallet, a soft-voiced, ardent devotee of Robert Duncan, H.D., and what she calls Trance Poetics, was the docent of our group of some dozen would-be dreamers. Kristin guided us through some exercises, including taking a book off the library shelves and seeing what we'd come up with, before we had milk and cookies and adjourned, though some people stayed up, talking quietly at the far end of the space. It took me a while to fall asleep, but then I had—as I often do—vivid dreams. Being awakened the next morning by Kristin's gentle, fierce voice reading aloud from H.D.'s "Hermetic Definition" was a memorable experience in itself. After a lavish buffet breakfast, we sat in a circle talking about dreams and reading some of our own poems, before packing up and heading out into the windy Sunday morning. No trick or treaters this time; the sky was the color of a bruise, and the trees by the river were tossing wildly. The hurricane was on the way.

Breitenbush

In November of last year, I spent two days at Breitenbush, a hot springs resort in Oregon, in the snowy Cascades. For several years, my husband's long and worsening dementia had made planning and traveling difficult. George died quite suddenly in October, and so just before Thanksgiving I went to Breitenbush with my son.

Any spa-type establishment has a Central European flavor: people come to relax, to get over ailments, to sweat out their stresses. Seeing all the nude bodies, one is reminded of figures depicted by Degas or Cézanne or Rubens. Since the pools we soak in are out of doors—the hot springs bubble up right out of the earth—one can look up at a willow branch overhead, or gaze across the valley to a snow-capped mountain, and find oneself in a Chinese scroll.

Wherever I go, even when I take my clothes off, I carry poems in my head, or I find them, or both. At the Breitenbush Lodge, where we had our meals (and which strongly reminded me of Colony Hall at MacDowell, where George and I met in 1976), there was a library. Browsing after dinner among walls of books on health and wellness and diet and spirituality of various stripes, I found a shelf of miscellaneous poetry books—Shakespeare, Donne, Keats—and then something more unexpected: *Four Penguin Poets* (1958), a slim paperback gathering of poetry for children by poets born late in the nineteenth century or early in the twentieth: Eleanor Farjeon, James Reeves, E. V. Rieu, and Ian Serraillier. Rieu I knew as a classicist and translator, but was not surprised to find he was also an accomplished poet of often wry verse. When Rieu writes about cats, though, the poems are heartbreaking. Back at the little cedar-scented cabin where we were sleeping, I copied 'The Lost Cat" and "Cat's Funeral" into my notebook. The final two stanzas of "Funeral" read:

> No more to watch bird stir;
> > No more to clean dark fur;
> No more to glisten as silk;
> No more to revel in milk;
> > No more to purr.
>
> Bury her deep, down deep;
> > She is beyond warm sleep.
> She will not walk in the night;
> She will not wake to the light.
> > Bury her deep.

Rieu uses monosyllables to chilling, authoritative effect: here is closure (not my favorite word) with a vengeance.

Digesting death—the death of a creature or a person with whom one has lived in intimacy and affection—isn't merely a matter of thumping finality. There was no Hart Crane on the Breitenbush poetry shelf, but lines from

Crane's early elegy "Praise for an Urn", which I hadn't looked at in years, kept shimmering and flickering in my head during the quiet soaks and rainy walks around the Breitenbush grounds. Crane's cubist technique in this poem, as he tries to reassemble his impressions and memories of a beloved teacher, speaks eloquently to how we laboriously process the fact of a recent death. Not only will the person (or cat) not eat or walk or wake to light, as in Rieu's elegy; but also we will not see them again. Crane's poetry is never easy, and "Praise for an Urn" is no exception. But the clearest lines in this poem, or at least the ones I found coming back to me, create fragmentary vignettes of the lost friend to whom the piece is dedicated. Here are three: "It was a kind and northern face;" "His thoughts, delivered to me / From the white coverlet and pillow"; and—most beautiful—"Still, having in mind gold hair . . .".

Weeks after George's death, I was only beginning to take in that I would not see his blue eyes or long hands again; that he would not enjoy life on earth again. The limitless modes of poetry match the limitless ways we grieve. Of all the myriad ways I or anyone floundering in the wake of a death might be feeling at a given moment, some poem will have captured the mood. Poems don't pose the well-meaning but impossibly unanswerable question "How are you?"; they're more likely to answer it. And when poems do ask questions—"Margaret, are you grieving / Over Goldengrove unleaving?"—it is not we who are being put on the spot.

Poems give mourners license to be inconsistent. Emily Dickinson has two poems that contradict one another. "They say that Time assuages" immediately asserts, in its second line, that "they" are wrong: 'Time never did assuage". Yet another poem asserts that "We grow accustomed to the dark," which I take to mean that yes, time does assuage, we do become habituated. Depending on when you happen to read them, both poems are telling the truth.

The titles of two of George's musical compositions are taken from poems: *Suave Mari Magno*, for solo piano, uses the phrase that opens Book II of *Lucretius' De Rerum Natura*. In this passage, Lucretius tells another truth that feels relevant when life presses on us: that when the sea is storm-tossed it is pleasant to stand on dry land and observe the troubles of others. "Moneta's Mourn," for orchestra, refers to the passage in Keats's "The Fall of Hyperion" where the veiled shade Moneta, stern but kind, confronts the dreaming narrator.

One of George's favorite poets was George Herbert, whose "The Flower" he set to music. "Who would have thought my shrivelled heart / Could have recovered greenness?" I used to read poems by Herbert and Hopkins and Whitman to this self-professed atheist in the years after he had become almost completely unable to speak—2010 and the first half of 2011, until the awful final spiral began. "You love Hopkins, remember?", I'd say. Or maybe I'd say: "You used to love Hopkins." And he would nod, and I would read, and sometimes my voice would break, but usually I got through the poem.

The last poem George set to music was Whitman's "This Compost," which begins "Something startles me where I thought I was safest"—another line that applies well to a mourner's sudden jolts of emotion. Just before Christmas, a curator in the Performing Arts Collection at the Rare Book and Manuscript Library at Columbia University showed me some of the collection's holdings. A late Whitman manuscript entitled "A Death Bouquet," "fresh pick'd noontime early January 1890," appears to be a little anthology of passages or poems about death Whitman liked. The last stanza of Tennyson's "Crossing the Bar" has been clipped apparently from a newspaper, and glued to the page. "Death," Whitman writes in pencil in a large and mostly legible hand, "—too great a subject to be treated so—indeed the greatest subject—and yet . . . . I am giving you but a few random lines . . . about it, as one writes hurriedly the last part of a letter to catch the closing mail."

QUESTIONS, QUESTIONS, QUESTIONS

Early in Michael Frayn and David Burke's *The Copenhagen Intrigue*, Frayn notes that

> I've had more letters about Copenhagen than about anything else I've ever written. There have been letters from scientists, historians, and philosophers... There have been moving letters from people who knew Heisenberg or the Bohrs... There have been poems from poets, plays from playwrights, enthusiasms from enthusiasts, madnesses from madmen.

And from students, whom Frayn omits from this catalog, there were undoubtedly lots of questions.

A mere poet, hardly the celebrated playwright and novelist Frayn is, I am nevertheless surely not alone among my poetic tribe in receiving a good many communications it would be pleasant but inaccurate to call fan mail. It isn't fan mail, it's email—specifically, emailed queries about my poems. Almost all the questioners are students who have encountered one of my poems, usually "The Red Hat," either in Advanced Placement high school English or in a college course. Often they have been asked or have chosen to report on a living poet and have selected me but don't know where to turn next.

I chose your poem, "The Red Hat." I have looked through a few sources so far but I could not find any critiques about the poem itself. I was wondering if you could perhaps assist me with the background of the poem.

As I imagine Frayn would agree, receiving messages about one's published work is an odd experience, not wholly unpleasant but not completely agreeable either. The poet Richard Wilbur, a remarkably gracious person, expresses well what I suspect is the ambivalence of many writers on this subject. On the one hand, he has written, he is

> gratified when people take the trouble to come out and hear me, or write and say that some lines of mine have mattered to them, and I think I owe their inquiries a civil response. After all, I too have questions to ask about poems which engage me, and the poets who wrote them.

Elsewhere, Wilbur observes that "we do inevitably treat a poem—in part—as the utterance of a person, and react to it as we would to a person." Nevertheless, he concedes ruefully that "there are indeed people who want to know not poetry but the poetry situation." And those are the folks who seem to be emailing me. Having been assigned to analyze or otherwise investigate a poem, they don't know any other approach than treating it as the utterance of a person in order to find out about "the poetry situation." So they turn to me.

Did you write it from personal experience? Is the main theme of separation the only theme? Is your personal psychology being expressed in this work? Any information would be greatly appreciated.

Why should this ruffle my feathers? Other writers, of whom Richard Wilbur is only one, seem to have taken it in stride. Umberto Eco received so many queries about the meaning of his international best-seller *The Name of the Rose* that he proceeded to write a little book on interpretation—not as sly as Frayn and Burke's *Copenhagen* confection, but sly enough. Eco claims cheerfully that

> nothing is of greater consolation to the author of a novel than the discovery of readings he had not conceived but which are then prompted by his readers....The large majority of readings reveal effects of sense that one had not thought of.

This point should hold for poems as well as novels. Eco here seems to be echoing from a novelist's perspective a comment Robert Frost made many years ago to the effect that the poet is entitled to whatever meaning the reader finds in his work. Still, and for me importantly, the fact that Eco welcomes fresh readings does not mean he is willing to answer any and all questions. Indeed, his stricture on this subject is one I have cited many times in answering students' queries about what I was trying to say: "The author must not interpret. But he may tell how and why he wrote his book."

Alas, students rarely suggest new readings of those poems of mine they find themselves studying. They do not very often even seek my own magisterial, authoritative interpretation. What then do they email me about? Soundbites, maybe, for their presentations on a living poet. Often they're in search of biographical or bibliographic facts which one would think were readily available in any good library, let alone online.

> Another part of our assignment is to provide a one page summary of biographical works [sic] as a whole. This part I am having a little bit of trouble with, because there is lots of information on your poems and novels but not on you. What I need is birth date and place of birth.

Since I have never written any novels, I wonder what information on them this student found.

In fairness, student often seem to encounter my poems out of context. I gather that teachers sometimes select, say, "The Red Hat" from one of the three anthologies in which it has appeared, and present it to the student with nothing but my name attached. But wait: isn't something like this pedagogical ploy—presenting the poem baldly, in isolation—what I.A. Richards documents in his ground-breaking 1929 study *Practical Criticism*? Richards explains his method as follows:

> For some years [as a lecturer at Cambridge and elsewhere] I have made the experiment of issuing printed sheets of poems—ranging in character from a poem by Shakespeare to a poem by Ella Wheeler Wilcox—to audiences who were requested to comment freely in writing upon them. The authorship of the poems was not revealed...

In concealing the authorship of the poems he taught, Richards went a step further than the rest of the group loosely labeled the New Critics. But the ideas about poetics broadly shared by Richards, Brooks, Warren, Tate, Empson, Eliot, and others all by and large steer the reader's attention away from the author and toward the text and only the text: its tensions and solutions, its tone and structure. "The 'prose-sense' of the poem," writes Brooks in *The Well Wrought Urn*, "is not a rack on which the stuff of the poem is hung." That was in 1947. In the last decades of the twentieth century, of course, the pendulum swung, not back toward the importance of the prose sense or the author's intention, but even farther away from them. Soon the author was declared irrelevant or dead; language itself was doing the writing.

In the meantime, though, technology had been advancing: the internet entered and transformed the student's arsenal of critical approaches. But you can't send a language, or a poem in it, an email message asking what it means; you need an author. Thus having been escorted out the door, we poets are creeping back in through the window. Students who have no idea how to analyze a poem are turning to the source—who else but the author? They have never heard the admonition to trust not the teller but the tale. If their search engines could locate Shakespeare or Keats, Dickinson or Ella Wheeler Wilcox, I have no doubt that students would be querying these members of the Dead Poets' Society too.

The emails I get are often polite and respectful; many apologize for bothering me and thank me in advance for my time. Some even express enthusiasm for my work: *I thoroughly enjoy your poem about the young boy "growing up."* All, however, share three interrelated assumptions:

1) In approaching a poem, the work's *what* trumps its *how.* Not only is content more accessible and more important than a vaguely defined and understood form; the latter is barely worth discussing.

2) Content (what Brooks sniffs is "the prose-sense of the poem") includes not only the plot or theme in the poem, but the elements in the poet's life which presumably gave rise to that plot or theme. If "The Red Hat" seems to be about a child's separation from its parents, then the poet must have a child and be writing about him or her. A successful analysis of the poem should include as many factual details as possible:

Is this an occurrence [sic] that happened to you? Was it one of your children? How old was the child when they first walked to school alone?

How far did the child have to walk by themself?

Is this poem autobiographical, and is the young boy your son?

Where is Straus Park located, is it near your home on West End mentioned in the poem?

3) The way to acquire such biographical details is to query the author, who if she takes the time can and will reliably report on not only facts but on such matters as what were your feelings when you wrote this? Is your personal psychology being expressed in this work? ... what different internal aspects went in to your completion of this piece?

My questioners felt an urgency in the poem's title, which they wanted to decode:

Why did you decide to name it the red hat instead of something else? Is there any significance in the red hat other than the child wearing it? What is the symbolism of the red hat? Other than the eponymous hat, though, no tropes seemed to send out any ripples. Formal matters like meter or rhyme, stanza or line breaks went unnoticed or at least unquestioned, though if the students had only known it, it is much easier for a poet (at least this poet) to reconstruct her decisions on technical matters than "personal psychology" at the time the poem was written. Come to think of it, I agree with only half of Eco's formulation: I'm happy to try to say *how* I wrote the poem. But not only will I not say *what* it means, I prefer not to analyze *why* I wrote it.

It's tempting, if unfair, to advert here to Alvin Kernan's morose comment in *The Death of Literature* that "the poetics of illiteracy...has performed...the standard institutional function of literary criticism." Kernan is probably overstating his case. Yet I fear that a more genial writer like the poet Edward Hirsch, who hopes that his own genuine love of the art will be contagious, commits hyperbole in the other direction. Hirsch's recent *How to Read a Poem and Fall in Love with Poetry* is rich in formulations like "The lyric poem is the most intimate and volatile form of literary discourse," or "the lyric poem seeks to mesmerize time. It crosses frontiers and outwits the temporal." Many readers and writers of poetry, including myself, will surely know what such statements mean and agree with them. But if outwitting the temporal, intimacy, volatility and so on mean that poems simply fly straight into our hearts and minds and nestle there, I fear that the students who have been emailing me about "The Red Hat" would shake their heads. Hirsch is closer to the mark, perhaps, when, shuffling his pack of metaphors, he writes that "the reader of poetry is a kind of pilgrim, setting forth." Yes, if the rod and the staff that comfort this pilgrim are email and its magical ability to enable the pilgrim to ask a poet what she means.

Of course it is pointless to lay the blame on email alone; much larger cultural trends are at work, and teachers have naturally caught on to them. We live in a time of the fast fix, a time that rewards surfing, browsing, skimming, the quick study. From AP exams to the SATS to quiz shows like *Jeopardy*, the eager student is encouraged to perform within the framework of the Q and A, spitting out answers (or questions) within an ever-shrinking time frame. I.A. Richards's students in the Twenties inhabited a world that was courtly and leisurely in comparison. Their minds may have been clogged, as Richards complains, with stock responses or mnemonic irrelevances, with inhibitions or sentimentality or even doctrinal adhesions, but most of them had probably read some poetry in secondary school and regarded the analysis of a poem as an occasion for thought, even if, like Paul Dombey's, their thoughts were mostly mush.

Sometime in the late Fifties, my father commented in a speech about the issue then known as the Two Cultures that a dictaphone was a very handy gadget on which to dictate a diatribe against technology. One wonders what use Richards and the other critics of his generation would make of email. It's all too easy to forget that the sheer ability of asking a stranger a question, reaching out toward another mind "With motion of no less celerity / Than that of thought" is a truly remarkable tool. A tool for literary analysis, though? Not as it's deployed by my students—not yet. For a start, someone needs to think up some better questions.

READING, WRITING, TEACHING, TIME:
A ROUND-TABLE DISCUSSION

Welcome to our ghostly round table discussion of the plight of the humanities. As I'm sure all of you in the audience are aware, the news has recently been pouring in on every side, from the American Academy of Arts and Sciences report on the humanities to the editorial pages of the New York Times to books such as Mark Bauerlein's The Dumbest Generation: How the Digital Age Stupefies Young Americans and Jeopardizes Our Future, to the effect that reading, writing, and teaching are all in big trouble in this country.

Rather than adding my personal testimony from thirty-odd years in a college classroom to these jeremiads, I thought I'd pull together a rather motley panel of experts in reading, writing, and teaching—experts who, although they may not always have been aware of the fact, turn out to be in conversation with one another. In the loops and meanders of their excerpted remarks, these panelists remind us that some of the problems hotly debated or lamented now aren't as new as we thought. This is not to say that we're not at a difficult juncture or that the effects of technology are less than cataclysmic. But it does suggest that classroom theory and practice, and perhaps also, as a result, the theory and practice of reading and writing outside the classroom, have always wavered and swung; have always been argued and debated and reacted against.

Another point I take away from our panelists' remarks is just how inextricably connected reading, writing, teaching, and also literary theory are. It's impossible to discuss either a classroom technique or a literary text without straying into the fields of psychology, epistemology, sociology, or neurology. Speaking of classrooms, I always enjoy poking my nose into someone else's classroom, whether real (that is, remembered) or imagined. Novelists turn out to be at least as good at conjuring up vivid classroom encounters as talking heads or task forces are.

I'm afraid our discussion may not reach any conclusions, but then neither do the lamentations that come pouring in daily reach conclusions. My hope, though, is that a few forgotten voices or nuggets of information from a past we seem to keep forgetting about will attract a little attention. At the very least, what follows may be enjoyable, before it too lands in what Orwell called the memory hole.

Panelists (in order of appearance, not chronology, and possibly including a few voices from the audience):

> Rachel Hadas, Moderator
> Verlyn Klinkenborg
> David Mikics

David Lehman
Willa Cather
Francisco Goldman
Andrew Delbanco
Task Force, Council on Foreign Relations
Charles Dickens
David Craig
Jeffrey Eugenides
Jean Howard
Reuben Brower
Anne Ferry
David Kalstone
Louise Bogan
Paula Marantz Cohen
Colm Toibin
E.M. Forster
Moses Hadas
Henry David Thoreau
John Ruskin
Nicholas Murray Butler

RH: Let me get the ball rolling by confessing that we could plunge into this sea of lamentation anywhere. I suggest we start with one or two reports from the front lines—the classrooms where reading and writing are actually taught (or not); or the quality of writing that is emerging from those classrooms, with the related matter of reading. Verlyn, you had something to say on this subject recently.

Verlyn Klinkenborg: In the past few years, I've taught nonfiction writing to undergraduates and graduate students at Harvard, Yale, Bard, Pomona, Sarah

Lawrence, and Columbia's Graduate School of
Journalism. Each semester I hope, and fear, that
I will have nothing to teach my students because
they already know how to write. And each semester
I discover, again, that they don't.

They can assemble strings of jargon and
generate clots of ventriloquistic syntax. They can
meta-metastasize any thematic or ideological
notion they happen upon. And they can get good
grades for doing just that. But as for writing clearly,
simply, with attention and openness to the world
around them—no.

RH: David Mikics can speak to this problem; he has
recently pointed out that all this ventriloquistic
syntax at which students are so proficient, all these
strings of jargon they so deftly assemble, constitute
prose that somebody presumably has to read. But
who (including English professors) has time?

David Mikics: Engulfed by a never-ending flood of text,
we barely have time to stop and reflect. Quick and
sloppy messages cascade around us constantly. This
tidal wave of bad writing, much of it demanding
a rapid response, gets in the way of true reading,
which takes time and concentration.

RH: It's impossible to disentangle technology from the
changes in reading and writing that we're seeing, or

any of these from the decline in the teaching of the humanities.

DM: The Internet has put everything in a new light: lightning-quick, yet blurry. The casual, makeshift sentence is now prized as more vital than the adept, finished one. Eloquence and careful elaboration seem mere time-wasters belonging to an older, less wired generation.

VK: Whenever I teach older students, whether they're undergraduates, graduate students or junior faculty, I find a vivid, pressing sense of how much they need the skill they didn't acquire earlier in life. They don't call that skill the humanities. They don't call it literature. They call it writing—the ability to distribute their thinking in the kinds of sentences that have a merit, even a literary merit, of their own.

Writing well used to be a fundamental principle of the humanities, as essential as the knowledge of mathematics and statistics in the sciences. But writing well isn't merely a utilitarian skill. It is about developing a rational grace and energy in your conversation with the world around you.

RH: Problems in reading and writing are not only inseparable from one another and from the extraordinary and ever accelerating technological changes of the past two decades. They're also inextricably bound up with what has happened to the way professors talk, and teach students to talk, about literature—ways Verlyn has already suggested.

David Lehman: A generation from now, literary historians are bound to regard our period with some wonderment. It was a time, they will note, when professors of literature solemnly subscribed to the doctrine that literature, while full of sound and fury, signifies nothing. It was a period when language turned in on itself—when the meaning or content of a piece of writing was deferred, or rendered "undecidable," or "problematized," while the scholars' energy went into close rhetorical readings of devious linguistic structures.

And I wrote that in 1991.

RH: I'm not sure the literary scholars these days are looking back on the early Nineties with wonderment. Rather, the atmosphere on campus or in the classroom, while in some ways streamlined by the speed of the Internet, has also become even more devious; rhetorical readings have become even closer. Those deconstructionists of the Eighties and Nineties might feel right at home in 2013.

VK: Studying the humanities should be like standing among colleagues and students on the open deck of a ship moving along the endless coastline of human experience. Instead, now it feels as though people have retreated to tiny cabins in the bowels of the ship, from which they peep out on a small fragment of what may be a coastline or a fog bank or the back of a spouting whale.

A technical narrowness, the kind of specialization and theoretical emphasis you might find in a graduate course, has crept into the undergraduate curriculum. That narrowness sometimes reflects the tight focus of a professor's research, but it can also reflect a persistent doubt about the humanistic enterprise. It often leaves undergraduates wondering, as I know from my conversations with them, just what they've been studying and why.

Willa Cather: If you ask me, this cautiousness about the humanistic enterprise, this technical narrowness, as Mr. Klinkenborg eloquently phrases it, are—at least in state universities—nothing new. I should know; I lived from 1873 to 1947. In my novel *The Professor's House*, which was published in 1925, the eponymous professor broods about the state of affairs at the university where he has long taught:

The State Legislature and the Board of Regents seemed determined to make a trade school of the university. Candidates for the degree of Bachelor of Arts were allowed credits for commercial studies;

courses in book-keeping, experimental farming, domestic science, dress-making, and what not. Every year the regents tried to diminish the number of credits required in science and the humanities. The liberal appropriations, the promotions and increases in salary, all went to professors who worked with the regents to abolish the purely cultural studies. Out of a faculty of sixty, there were perhaps twenty who made any serious stand for scholarship, and [he] was one of the staunchest.

He had lost the Deanship of the College of Science because of his uncompromising opposition to the degrading influence of politicians in university affairs. The honor went, instead, to a much younger man, head of the department of chemistry, who was willing "to give the taxpayers what they wanted."

RH: Thank you for that historical perspective, Miss Cather. Hmmm, *plus ça change.* I'm not sure whether it's interesting or depressing to note that "cultural studies" in the 1920's was a field full of humanist frippery it was thought desirable to abolish. The term means something very different now. For example, in the early 2000's—well, let's hear how Francisco Goldman's novel *Say Her Name* describes the Spanish Department at Columbia University.

Francisco Goldman: Professors who still taught novels and poetry in their classes were being forced out.

Specialists in critical theory and cultural studies
were taking over. Aura had unwittingly enrolled in
a department where a purge was under way. The
department was finally, belatedly modernizing...
Where was it written that every department that
taught Spanish owed a special allegiance to fiction
and poetry?

RH: The testimonies from Mssrs. Klinkenborg and
Goldman, not to mention the deep background
provided by Miss Cather, all tend to confirm
Andrew Delbanco's eloquent unease about the
humanities as they are taught in colleges today.

Andrew Delbanco: Literature, history, philosophy,
and the arts are becoming the stepchildren of our
colleges. This is a great loss, because they are the
legatees of religion in the sense that they provide
a vocabulary for formulating ultimate questions
of the sort that have always had a special urgency
for young people. In fact, the humanities may have
the most to offer to students who do not know they
need them—which is one reason it is scandalous to
withhold them. One of the ironies of contemporary
academic life is that even as the humanities become
marginal in our colleges, they are establishing
themselves in medical, law, and business schools,
where interest is growing in the study of literature
and the arts as a way to encourage self-critical
reflection.

RH: Andy, I'm interested that you and the other
panelists do not include creativity among the
desirable qualities fostered by an education in the
humanities. Curiosity, reflection, contemplation—
yes, by all means. Maybe we'll loop back to curiosity
later, if we manage to touch upon the issue of what
kind of questions students and teachers should ask
of texts. But the advocacy of creativity and also
imagination, however those terms are understood,
tends to come these days from unexpected sources.
Here for example is the Council on Foreign
Relations 2012 report, "U.S. Education Reform
and National Security." The prose, as is clear, was
written by a committee.

Task Force, Council on Foreign Relations: The Task
Force believes that all young people—those who
aim to work in national security and those who
aim to work in corporations or not-for-profit
corporations—must develop their imaginations
from an early age. This is increasingly important
as information becomes more and more abundant
and as the world becomes more interconnected
and complex. The United States has traditionally
led the world in patent applications, invention, and
innovation. The Task Force members believe that to
retain this important competitive edge, lessons in
creativity—whether in the arts or creative analysis
or imaginative problem solving, must begin in early

elementary school.

RH: Creativity turns out to be closely linked to invention and innovation in the context of competition. Education turns out to be instrumental, severely pragmatic; improving student performance whether in math and science or in the undefined area of creativity serves the cause of maintaining our country's "important competitive edge."

VK: Undergraduates will tell you that they're under pressure—from their parents, from the burden of debt they incur, from society at large—to choose majors they believe will lead as directly as possible to good jobs. Too often, that means skipping the humanities. In other words, there is a new and narrowing vocational emphasis in the way students and their parents think about what to study in college.

RH: But as I'm sure Miss Cather would agree, this vocational emphasis, though its locale and rationale have shifted somewhat, is nothing new either. Mr. Dickens, maybe you'll read us the beginning of Chapter Two of your 1854 novel, *Hard Times*. This chapter, which is entitled "Murdering the Innocents," takes us into a classroom.

Charles Dickens: Thomas Gradgrind, sir. A man of realities. A man of fact and calculations. A man who proceeds upon the principle that two and two are four, and nothing over, and who is not to be talked into allowing for anything over....With a rule and a pair of scales, and the multiplication table always in his pocket, sir, ready to weigh and measure any parcel of human nature, and tell you exactly what it comes to. It is a mere question of figures, a case of simple arithmetic....In such terms Mr. Gradgrind always mentally introduced himself....In such terms...substituting the words 'boys and girls', for 'sir,' Thomas Gradgrind now presented Thomas Gradgrind to the little pitchers before him, who were to be filled so full of facts....he seemed a kind of cannon loaded with facts, and prepared to blow them clean out of the regions of childhood at one discharge. He seemed a galvanizing apparatus, too, charged with a grim mechanical substitute for the tender young imaginations that were to be stormed away.

RH: A little later in the chapter, a new pupil named Sissy Jupe, the daughter of a horse-trainer, fails to define "horse" with the requisite degree of abstraction, so Mr. Gradgrind calls on a boy named Bitzer. Is it a coincidence that the star pupil Bitzer, in Dickens's memorable description, seems part albino and part reptile or insect?

CD: The square finger, moving here and there, lighted suddenly on Bitzer, perhaps because he chanced

to sit in the same ray of sunlight which, darting
in at one of the bare windows of the intensely
whitewashed room, irradiated Sissy. For, the boys
and girls sat on the face of the inclined plane in two
compact bodies, divided up the centre by a narrow
interval; and Sissy, being at the corner of a row
on the sunny side, came in for the beginning of a
sunbeam, of which Bitzer, being at the corner of a
row on the other side...caught the end. But, whereas
the girl was so dark-eyed and dark-haired, that
she seemed to receive a deeper and more lustrous
colour from the sun when it shone upon her, the
boy was so light-eyed and light-haired that the
self-same rays appeared to draw out of him what
little colour he ever possessed. His cold eyes would
hardly have been eyes, but for the short ends of
lashes which, by bringing them into immediate
contrast with something paler than themselves,
expressed their form. His short-cropped hair
might have been a mere continuation of the sandy
freckles on his forehead and face. His skin was so
unwholesomely deficient in the natural tinge that
he looked as though, if he were cut, he would bleed
white.

'Bitzer,' said Thomas Gradgrind. 'Your definition
of a horse.'

'Quadruped. Graminivorous. Forty teeth,
namely twenty-four grinders, four eye-teeth,
and twelve incisive. Sheds coat in the spring; in
marshy countries, sheds hoofs too. Hoofs hard, but

requiring to be shod with iron. Age known by marks
in mouth.' Thus (and much more) Bitzer.

'Now, girl number twenty,' said Mr. Gradgrind.
'You know what a horse is.'

She curtseyed again, and would have blushed
deeper, if she could have blushed deeper than
she had blushed all this time. Bitzer, after rapidly
blinking at Thomas Gradgrind with both eyes at
once, and so catching the light upon his quivering
ends of lashes that they looked like the antennae
of busy insects, put his knuckles to his freckled
forehead, and sat down again.

RH: This creepily vivid scene looks like Dickensian
exaggeration. But apparently, apart (one assumes)
from the allegorically appropriate coloring
of the two students, Dickens was drawing on
contemporary educational practice.

David Craig, editor of Penguin edition of *Hard Times*:
The Gradgrind model school with its regimen of
pure fact is in no way an allegory or symbol of
what a cult of fact would run to if carried to an
extreme....The fact is that the first two chapters
of [*Hard Times*] are an almost straight copy of the
teaching system in schools run by...societies for
educating the poor. In the Manchester Lancasterian
School a thousand children were taught in one
huge room, controlled by a kind of military drill
with monitors and a monitor-general, and taught

by methods derived from the Cathechism. Groups of facts, mechanically classified, were drummed in by methods that might have been meant to squash forever the children's urge to find out or understand anything for themselves...

A lesson on natural history would be given thus. The boys would read: ruminating animals. Cud-chewing or ruminating animals form the *eighth* order...

This of course is precisely Bitzer's "Quadruped. Graminivorous..." and so on....Given this kind of thing Dickens had no need to invent: the satire was already there in life, and not on some lunatic fringe but in a widespread, dominant, and much-admired system.

RH: Whether or not Dickens was inventing Bitzer's definition of a horse, it often seems to be the novelists, as much as or more than cultural commentators, who succeed in taking us right inside the classroom. I'd love to be a fly on the wall in the kind of class envisioned (or not envisioned) by the Task Force writers, with their emphasis on "creative analysis" and "imaginative problem-solving." One vivid scene in a novel can sometimes capture the unease expressed by numerous editorial writers.

My favorite scenes from Jeffrey Eugenides's 2012 novel *The Marriage Plot* are the ones which take us into Semiotics 211, a cutting-edge class at Brown in the 1980's. Eugenides evokes the glamour this new field offers English majors.

Jeffrey Eugenides: ...if scanning Wordsworth was making you feel dowdy and ink-stained, there was another option. You could flee...the old New Criticism. You could sign up for Semiotics 211 and find out what everyone else was talking about.

RH: A strange coincidence, if that's what it is, links Eugenides's depiction of a Semiotics 211 seminar and Dickens's evocation of the classroom where Bitzer defines a horse. Just as Sissy Jupe is healthy-looking whereas Bitzer is ghostly, so Madeleine, the heroine of *The Marriage Plot*, stands out for her unfashionable wholesomeness.

JE: Everyone in the room was so spectral-looking that [her] natural healthiness seemed suspect, like a vote for Reagan.

RH: Doesn't Sissy's natural healthiness also seem suspect, as if it underlines her common-sensical nature? The resemblance that really struck me when I read about these two very different classrooms links the pallid Bitzer with Madeleine's classmate Thurston Meems, who has shaved his eyebrows (compare Bitzer's pale lashes) and who tells the class:

JE: "I read *Of Grammatology* last summer and it blew my mind."

RH: I also enjoyed the taste of classroom etiquette, or culture, or whatever one calls it, suggested by the fact that Thurston finds...

JE: "...it is hard to introduce myself, actually, because the whole idea of social introductions is so problematized."

RH: So that not shaving your eyebrows, not having a hard time introducing yourself, wanting to define a horse based on your experience rather than factual paradigms—all these impulses or attitudes seem unfashionably, uncoolly commonsensical. Smart students like Bitzer and Thurston often bend themselves into the shapes their professors, or the latest trends, seem to require. As I've said, just what those shapes are is much easier to glean from a fictional evocation of a classroom than from the hopelessly abstract and clumsy language of (for example) the Task Force report.

WC and CD: Pardon our ignorance, but we aren't familiar with the term "Semiotics." And though we have both read Wordsworth, we are unsure what "the old New Criticism" means, though we think we know what "old," "new," and "criticism" denote.

RH: It's always salutary to admit you don't know what someone is talking about, so thank you, Miss Cather and Mr. Dickens. The New Criticism—well, I could begin in the middle by saying that it has been vehemently reacted against in recent years. For example, a Columbia University scholar of Early Modern (as they now call it) literature reportedly admonishes her students...

Jean Howard: Don't fetishize the text!

RH: Speaking of texts, maybe we need to go back to some of the tenets of a formalist approach to the study of literature, as set forth in an essay about teaching poetry in a college literature course. Formalism, by the way, a term that suggests close readings of texts, is one way of categorizing the New Criticism, which (in case you're wondering) was called new in the 1940's and 50's because it in turn was reacting against other, older ways of approaching literature. As we've already seen with ideas about imagination or facts in classrooms, there's a general principle that the pendulum swings back and forth.

Reuben Brower, Anne Ferry, and David Kalstone: We begin with short poems because they offer literary experience in its purest form. By beginning with poems we can be reasonably sure that the student learns early to distinguish between life and literature without being unduly distracted by questions of biography and history or by social and psychological problems of the type raised so often by the novel. Most important, the student will learn at the outset to deal with wholes, since within the limits of a class–hour or a brief paper he can arrive at an interpretation of a whole literary expression. Poems may come to stand in his mind as Platonic forms of true and complete literary experience.

RH: A key idea expressed here can be found in that interesting language "unduly distracted by questions of biography and history or by social and psychological problems of the type raised so often by the novel." It isn't merely a matter of privileging (a verb Brower, Ferry, and Kalstone, let alone Cather and Dickens, were probably unfamiliar with) one genre, poetry, over another, fiction. The fundamental distinction between life and literature, the sense that literature should be studied in a "pure" form, is a basic New Critical tenet. Poems should be allowed to speak as "true and complete" in themselves.

autotellic

Louise Bogan: To sandwich poems between great slabs of interpretation, quotation, appreciation, and adulation is wearing to anyone who believes that practically nothing...should be interspersed between the reader and the poem...It is fine to be a liaison officer, though combining preacher, teacher, and special pleader with liaison officer can become rather tiresome to all concerned.

RH: This notion of the separation of text from history, or of de-sandwiching the poem from between the slabs of critical reception, is often anathema these days to the practitioners of literary studies and their students, especially now that cultural studies (the meaning of the term has changed, Miss Cather), queer theory, post-Colonial studies, disability studies, and so on loom so large in the field of literature. Such approaches are implied in Verlyn Klinkenborg's point about ideological notions that students so deftly insert into their prose. In many ways, the emphasis in classrooms seems to have shifted from the text to issues around the text—those doughy slabs that poet-critic Louise Bogan found wearisome a generation ago. And yet engaging closely with texts continues to be an irreplaceable classroom technique. Paula Marantz Cohen has recently blogged eloquently about some of her experiences teaching a class in British literature; the specific text was Wordsworth's *The Prelude.*

Paula Marantz Cohen: We proceeded to spend a class period discussing...seven lines...You may argue that I had reverted to the New Critical method that had already begun to be out-of-date when I graduated from college in 1975. Of course I had; all good teaching grapples with the particulars of the text. But the approach wasn't just close reading in the hermeneutical sense; it was also about familiarizing students with the language and style of the work, explaining the use of enjambment and caesura as these elements give the poem its vital connection to natural speech, and discussing Wordsworth's intimate feeling for nature...and his profound appreciation for, and possible fear of, solitude. We discussed the mood that the poet was after and correlated it with experiences in our own lives that had given rise to a similar mood.

RH: Furthermore, even now, critics of the novel who are themselves novelists (or poets, as we've seen with Bogan) often stress the pattern or texture of the novel as an art form rather than "being unduly distracted by questions of biography and history or by social and psychological problems of the type raised so often by the novel."

Colm Toibin: The novel is not a moral fable or a tale from the Bible, or an exploration of the individual's role in society; it is not our job to like or dislike characters in fiction, or make judgments on their worth, or learn from them how to live. We can do that with real people and, if we like, figures from history. They are for moralists to feast on. A novel is a pattern and it is our job to relish and see clearly its textures and its tones, to notice how the textures were woven and the tones put into place.

RH: Having said this, Colm, you then distance yourself a bit from the formalist stance and claim some sort of middle ground.

CT: This is not to insist that a character in fiction is merely a verbal construct and bears no relation to the known world. It is rather to suggest that the role of a character in a novel must be judged not as we would judge a person. Instead, we must look for density, for weight and strength within the pattern, for ways in which figures in novels have more than one easy characteristic, one simple affect. A novel is a set of strategies, closer to something in mathematics or quantum physics than something in ethics or sociology. It is a release of certain energies and a dramatization of how these energies might be controlled, given shape.

RH: Colm, I wonder if you aren't taking a page from E.M. Forster's *Aspects of the Novel* (1927), which devotes a chapter to "Pattern and Rhythm." Forster's discussion of pseudo-scholarship in his "Introductory" chapter, still relevant in 2013, distinguishes between scholars who "can contemplate the river of time" and the pseudo-scholar, who "classes books before he has understood or read them; that is his first crime."

E.M. Forster: Classification by chronology. Books written before 1847, books written after it, books written after or before 1848. The novel in the reign of Queen Anne, the pre-novel, the ur-novel, the novel of the future. Classification by subject matter—sillier still.

RH: Talk about being unduly distracted by questions of biography and history! Colm Toibin and E.M. Forster, both wonderful novelists, are more interested in what might be called the New Critical or formalist approach to the study of literature— what Paula Marantz Cohen calls (and Brower, Ferry, and Kalstone would agree) the language and style of the work. One way I like to pose the distinction for students is to ask them to consider that the how in literature (voice, style, diction, structure, rhythm) generally trumps the what (content, ideas, what used to be called theme when I was in high school). Of course if we ignore the what entirely, we do so at our peril. And when the text in question isn't fiction or poetry but a work of literary theory or philosophical discourse, the absence of a what can be dizzying. In Jeffrey Eugenides's *The Marriage Plot*, when the heroine, Madeleine, asks

JE: what *Of Grammatology* was about, she was given to understand...that the idea of a book being "about" something was exactly what this book was against, and that, if it was "about" anything, then it was about the need to stop thinking of books as being about things.

RH: It's interesting that Madeleine has—at least initially—the courage to ask what a book is about. In the whole inchoate business of reading and writing, education and creativity and imagination, which questions are asked is an important and often glossed-over issue. I have in mind not only the "ultimate questions" Andrew Delbanco mentions, which often arise in the context of discussions of the humanities (Paula Marantz Cohen also attests to this), but the kinds of text-related questions David Mikics discusses in his very interesting fourteen rules for slow reading. David, your second rule is: Ask the Right Questions.

DM: When you read a book, think of yourself as a detective looking for clues. Any good detective needs to know what's relevant and what's not, which leads should be followed up and which go nowhere. Detectives are masters at figuring out which questions will move an investigation forward and which ones won't. Asking questions is how you get from perplexity to engagement....Useful questions connect elements of a book together: What does the beginning have to do with the ending? How do the characters argue or balance against one another? What does a particularly striking passage sum up about the book as a whole?

RH: These useful questions are in the formalist tradition in that they ask us to look harder at the text. I find it helpful, David, that you also discuss questions that are not useful to ask about literary texts.

DM: There are some questions that can be asked and answered on a first reading, others that might be addressed later on, and, finally, questions that the book can't answer. I call this last kind of question a false lead (to return to the idea of detective work). You won't get very far inventing a prequel to Hamlet depicting the prince's relationship with his father. Shakespeare has deliberately withheld this story, for a reason: he wants the connection between *Hamlet* and his father to remain uncertain, fraught, and challenging.

You're asking the right questions about a literary work if your questions always lead you back to the book you have in hand, rather than taking you away from it into the realms of politics or history....Asking questions about historical background will give you a way of making sense of the story you are reading, if that story alludes to what really happened in history. But make sure that you are not using the facts of history to simplify the meaning of a work, to reduce it to the author's expression of a political opinion. Writers of literary works rarely take up positions about the events of their time, even when they discuss these events closely; literature can't be translated into political position-taking.

RH: In maybe a subtler or more nuanced way, David is re-presenting some of the arguments Brower, Ferry, and Kalstone, among others, made back in the Sixties for focusing on texts. As Paula Marantz Cohen reminds us, this "New Critical method had already begun to be out-of-date...in 1975." But the pendulum swings, as we've seen. Sometime in the late Fifties or early Sixties, my father Moses Hadas (1900-1966) wrote a talk, never published, "On Teaching Classics in Translation." I like the distinction he draws between teaching a book and teaching about, or around, a text.

Moses Hadas: The first rule, especially hard for teachers fresh from graduate school to apply, is to teach the book, not about the book. It is easier to lecture about the time and place of a book, the culture that produced it, the special historical or linguistic problems involved in it. It is harder, but more to our purpose, to face the book as a masterpiece and to help the student understand why it is a masterpiece....If you dodge the book and conceal your fecklessness by loud noises in the outworks, the whole enterprise becomes fraudulent. There are crambooks from which your students can get all the knowledge you purvey with their bare feet on a table.

RH: Daddy, I love that weirdly prescient vision, feet on the table and all, of Google or Wikipedia or Spark Notes. Did you maybe envision open laptops as well as bare feet? I also love that you acknowledge how tempting such short cuts are. Now, of course, the loud noises in the outworks and the crambooks you mention are all available effortlessly, at the click of a mouse.

MH: I emphasize this point because I find it needs to be impressed on all instructors in our Humanities course, and not least myself. I would cheerfully undertake an hour's discourse on any author included in my history of literature courses without preparation; I would not dare to enter a Humanities course without first trying to recover the excitement of a first unprofessional reading.

DM: Once, when I was teaching Nietzsche to a freshman class, a student told me that if she continued to read Nietzsche's *Toward the Genealogy of Morals* she would have to question everything she had ever believed. She said this with trepidation, but with a thrill, too. Even if you're no longer in college, you should cultivate the same aliveness when you read books like Nietzsche's, which call on you to rethink your life and the whole world you live in.

AD: It will always be hard to state the value of ...[a humanist] education in a succinct or summary way. Yet many people, if given half a chance, discover it for themselves.

Henry David Thoreau: There are probably words addressed to our condition exactly, which, if we could really hear and understand, would be more salutary than the morning or the spring to our lives, and possibly put a new aspect on the face of things for us. How many a man has dated a new era in his life from the reading of a book. The book exists for us perchance which will explain our miracles and reveal new ones.

RH: If readers don't have the brilliance and serendipity of a reader like Thoreau (and who does?), college syllabi should help them discover the right works, and rules like David's can help them to be attentive, to be open, maybe above all (David's first rule) to be patient.

John Ruskin: There is a society continually open to us of people who will talk to us as long as we like, whatever our rank or occupation—talk to us in the best words they can choose, and of the things nearest their hearts. They can be kept waiting round us all day long.

RH: But although books are patient, and readers can

learn to be patient too, teachers should be more realistic about how much reading material they assign.

Paula Marantz Cohen: My...strategy was to be extremely careful about how much material I assigned. If the work was especially challenging, then it was important to dole out the reading in small increments, at least in the beginning, and to start by reading the piece aloud and discussing both the style and the meaning of the opening pages. Since it is obvious that reading a few sentences together with a class can ease the way and make a text much less daunting, it is a wonder that more teachers don't do this on a regular basis.

DM: How you read matters much more than how much you read.

RH: And yet, though David doesn't bring up this point, there is, or there used to be, such a thing as reading (or teaching) a text too slowly—a way of approaching a literary work that seems to foster pedantry rather than reward patience, and that seems connected, too, to asking the wrong kinds of questions about a work—although in the case we're about to hear, the wrong questions pertain not to history and politics but to grammar. My father attests to the experience, in a Columbia classroom in 1879, of a classical scholar of the generation

previous to his, Nicholas Murray Butler, who went
on to become President of Columbia University.

Nicholas Murray Butler: ...the teaching of the classics
in those days was almost wholly of that dry-as-
dust type which has pretty nearly killed classical
study in the United States. Professor Drisler, who
was then Jay Professor [of Greek], was a man of
remarkable elevation of character and of mind
as well as a sound and thorough scholar. He was,
however, so given to insistence upon the minutest
details of grammar that our eyes were kept closely
fixed on the ground and we hardly ever caught
any glimpse of the beauty and larger significance
of the great works upon which we were enaged.
For example, I recall that during the first term
of sophomore year we were to read with Doctor
Drisler the *Medea* of Euripides and that when the
term came to an end we had completed but 246
lines. In other words, we never came to know
what the *Medea* was all about or to see either the
significance of the story of the quality of its literary
art.

MH: Perhaps the best testimonial to the worth and
viability of the classics is that they somehow
survived such treatment.

NMB: In Latin Professor Charles Short was a pedant if

there ever was one....whether he was dealing with Horace, with Juvenal or with Tacitus, he was always attending to the less important matters which the study of these authors suggested.

RH: In graduate school, Butler experienced more of the same kind of teaching.

NMB: In addition to my graduate study of philosophy I continued my work in Greek and Latin, getting some glorious experiences from my study of Plato but finding little benefit from the work given me by Professor Short. How unimportant his work was for my particular intellectual interest may be seen from a very technical philological paper which I contributed at Professor Gildersleeve's request to the *American Journal of Philology* in October 1885, with the title "The Post-Positive Et in Propertius."

RH: Modes of scholarly approach change, but it's safe to say that students still submit to scholarly journals articles whose topics have been suggested by their professors. Also, the pace of change is pretty slow. When I was a Harvard classics major in the late 1960's, our Greek class read *Oedipus the King* for what I remember as a whole semester; we didn't finish the play, and we mostly attended to grammar, as I recall. Our professor was a Latinist and Vergil scholar, Wendell Clausen, who didn't seem especially interested in Sophocles. Maybe Cedric Whitman or John Finley were on sabbatical.

We students, of course, never uttered a peep.

By the time I got to Princeton, things had changed in a way. A graduate course in Greek lyric poetry promised a taste of Sappho, but I was discouraged in the first seminar to hear about nothing but Lacan. Again, no one protested. But I dropped the course.

But to return to Nicholas Murray Butler's student experiences as recounted by my father; the flavor of pedantry that evidently reigned in the field of philology in the 1870's was associated not with French theory (that came later) but with a kind of slowness and thoroughness that actually discouraged students from seeing a text (say a Greek play) as a whole; all trees, or even all veins on the leaves, no forest. The New Critical emphasis on wholes, as mentioned by Brower, Ferry, and Kalstone, somehow got lost on the way to the post-positive *Et* in Propertius.

So that if a scholar like Moses Hadas was daring enough to move quickly through a text, even, or especially, a text in translation, as was done in the Columbia Colloquium, which eventually became the Humanities Core Curriculum, it was something of a scholarly scandal.

MH: Professional philosophers and philologians who take a year for the *Republic* are outraged that we dispatch it in a week. If the students' reading is superficial, any honest scholar will admit that his is also, and the *Republic* was not intended as a preserve for professors.

DM: Years ago, I taught a course with an older colleague from whom I learned an enormous amount about teaching, and about reading. We were beginning to study Plato's *Republic*, all six hundred dense pages of it. My colleague began his lecture with a single sentence: "Plato is smarter than you." We are not necessarily convinced that our friends are much smarter than we are; if we were so convinced, we might be too intimidated to talk to them. But books, if they are truly worthwhile, are smarter. We must be willing to learn from their authors, who know much more than we do. We must patiently try to understand an author's argument before we share our own opinion, before we start talking back.

RH: Maybe there's a happy medium between never raising one's eyes from the footnotes and the *hapax legomena* on the one hand, and talking around a text on the other—that is, providing biographical and historical and theoretical information, Marx and Lacan and Sedgwick and Fanon and Said, at the expense of the words on the page. Every teacher has to find this pedagogical balance somehow—and it's a personal and temperamental balance as well as a teacherly one.

MH: If you dodge the book and conceal your fecklessness

by loud noises in the outworks, the whole enterprise becomes fraudulent.

RH: Yes, you've said that before, but I think it bears repeating, because the current loud noises in the outworks, or the crambooks you also mentioned, have all been amplified and speeded up by technology. Now the crambooks are available at the click of a mouse; the loud noises which now talk around or over or behind the book instead of about the book tend to be ideological in nature, and students are usually as obedient in following their teachers' lead in 2013 as they were in 1879. Think of Bitzer in *Hard Times*, or Thurston Meems in *The Marriage Plot*, or the eager-beaver students waving their hands in classrooms ranging from the one George Orwell unforgettably describes in "Such, Such Were the Joys" to Hogwarts.

Bibliography of Works Cited

Louise Bogan, *A Poet's Alphabet* (New York: McGraw-Hill, 1970).

Reuben A. Brower, Anne Ferry, and David Kalstone, ed., *Beginning with Poems* (New York: Norton, 1966).

Nicholas Murray Butler, *Across the Busy Years: Recollections and Reflections* (New York: Scribners, 1939).

Willa Cather, *The Professor's House* (New York: Vintage, 1973).

Paula Marantz Cohen, "The Seduction," *The American Scholar* (Winter 2011).

David Craig, introduction to *Hard Times* by Charles Dickens (New York: Penguin Classics, 1969).

Andrew Delbanco, *College: What It Was, Is, and Should Be* (Princeton: Princeton University Press, 2012).

Charles Dickens, *Hard Times* (New York: Penguin Classics, 1969).

Jeffrey Eugenides, *The Marriage Plot* (New York: Farrar Straus Giroux, 2011).

E.M. Forster, *Aspects of the Novel* (New York: Harvest, 1954).

Francisco Goldman, *Say Her Name* (New York: Grove, 2011).

Moses Hadas, *Old Wine, New Bottles: A Humanist Teacher at Work* (New York: Simon and Schuster, 1962).

Moses Hadas, "On Teaching Classics in Translation" (unpublished talk)

Verlyn Klinkenborg, "Decline and Fall of the English Major," *New York Times,* June 22, 2013.

David Lehman, *Signs of the Times* (New York: Simon and Schuster, 1991).

David Mikics, *Slow Reading in a Hurried Age* (Cambridge: Harvard University Press, 2013).

John Ruskin, *Of Kings' Treasuries* (London: 1865)

Henry David Thoreau, *Walden* (Boston: Beacon Press, 1997).

Colm Toibin, *New Ways to Kill Your Mother* (New York: Scribners, 2012).

ALAN ANSEN

I hadn't thought about Alan Ansen for some time, before I met him again the other day—in disguise—while flicking through a copy of *On the Road*. Ansen appears in Kerouac's novel as Rollo Greb. "That Rollo Greb is the greatest, most wonderful of all. That's what I was trying to tell you—that's what I want to be. He's never hung-up, he goes every direction, he lets it all out, he knows time . . . ." Ansen also turns up as AJ in *Naked Lunch*, and as Dad Deform in Gregory Corso's only novel, *American Express*. His own work is preserved in *Contact Highs: Selected Poems 1957-1987*, published in 1989. In the same year, Sea Cliff Press issued *The Table Talk of W. H. Auden*, edited by Nicholas Jenkins but quarried from records meticulously kept by Ansen, a lifelong journal keeper. Alan met Auden in 1946 when the latter was lecturing on Shakespeare at the New School in New York. Before long, Alan had become Auden's secretary, and they remained lifelong friends.

I met Alan in Athens in October 1969. I arrived armed with a letter of introduction—a phrase that smacks of the nineteenth century, or earlier—to James Merrill from John Hollander, and it was John who also pointed me in the direction of Alan. I don't remember much of our first meeting, but the tall old house on Alopekis Street where he lived remains vivid. Alan had an apartment there, as did another American expatriate and poet, Bernie Winebaum, and there were other tenants. The arrangement of the house, with its central courtyard, reminded me of the description of the Hotel de Guermantes, where Jupien and Charlus have an encounter in the *Sodom and Gomorrah* volume of *Á la Recherche du temps perdu*.

Alan's apartment was notable for innumerable books and vases full of tall flowers—gladiolas, in particular. He bought the flowers fresh each week at the *Laiki agora*, a few blocks up the hill which turned into Mount Lykavettos, but he never changed the water, so towards the end of the week there was often a ripe, moldy smell in his living room—a smell which may also have derived from some of the books. The Friday market makes an appearance in Merrill's poem "Days of 1964": "Next, I was crossing a square / In which a moveable outdoor market's / Vegetables, chickens, pottery kept materializing / Through a dream-press of hagglers." The most striking pictures on Alan's wall were a big Cocteau line drawing of something with a tenderly bent, horned head—a faun? a unicorn?—and two elaborate, colorful collages by Corso. He used tiny pieces of gold paper among other colors, so the collages had a vaguely mosaic or stained-glass ecclesiastical look. Who knows where all of Alan's paintings are now?

There were two sofas in the flower and book–filled living room, hard and covered with grubby tapestries, but very comfortable. My little apartment up the hill was lonely, and I started spending a lot of time on those sofas. We had dinner most nights with Auden's companion Chester Kallman, who lived a few blocks away. Chester would phone Alan in the morning with a list of ingredients and Alan would duly go shopping. "*Kali routina*, Alan," Merrill used to say. The cocktails were served in Alan's big wine glasses, which were as cloudy as the flower water, followed by plenty of wine.

By early in the New Year, Alan and I were reading a bit of Dante every day—or rather I was, with Alan's patient and histrionic help. I remember his dramatically pathetic rendition of Dante's plaintive admission to Vergil, "*Io non Eneo, io non Paolo sono.*" We got as far as the *Purgatorio*, and I drew a picture of one of the allegorical pageants to get it straight in my mind's eye. He had a sensible policy of not lending anything from his library, but the contents of many of his books, in any case, seemed to be in his head; he recited, declaimed and burst (in the case of operas) into song.

Alan lived books, in a way that was rare even then. And he was a natural teacher. My bookish childhood and my recent years at Harvard as a classics major had left me almost totally ignorant of modern literature. I wrote poetry and had been poetry editor of the *Harvard Advocate*, but knew next to nothing about twentieth-century poetry. In March 1970, Alan gave me a copy of John Fuller's *Reader's Guide to W. H. Auden*. I know the date because he inscribed it, with the message "A cart before a heavenly horse."

This formulation strikes me now as not only tactful but true of the ways in which we often encounter literature. How many undergraduates first meet Dante when they read "The Lovesong of J. Alfred Prufrock," or encounter Baudelaire or Wagner in *The Waste Land*. After that, it's a matter of playing catch-up. Alan's lordly assumption that everyone knew as much as he did was perhaps a pose, perhaps a hopeful stance; but the warm-hearted inscription to the Fuller book shows he knew perfectly well how ignorant I was.

Notwithstanding the *Selected Poems* (there are also several self-published books of poetry), there is something essentially fugitive about Alan's presence in the literary record. In his introduction to Auden's *Table Talk*, Richard Howard writes: "An accomplished and singular poet, Ansen has chosen to edit himself out of the picture more sedulously than even the promptings of a pursued conversation would imply." There is a famous photograph taken in Tangier in 1961, with Corso, William Burroughs, Allen Ginsberg, Peter Orlovsky and Paul Bowles. A young man called Ian Somerville stands on the right. Between him and a bit behind Ginsberg and Corso, almost obscured by their bodies, stands Alan. On the back of his first book of poetry, *Disorderly Houses* (1961), we find the following, probably written by Alan: "Of the poet himself, there is little that may be said. He is one who believes that a man's private life should remain private except as it may be revealed by his works. Let it be stated, then, that he is an American who finds it congenial to live abroad and who is able to do so. For the rest, let his poems speak for themselves."

Disorderly Houses is dedicated to Auden and Burroughs, and Alan can be regarded as an odd hybrid of these divergent literary lineages. The idiom of the poems is neither the language of confessionalism nor of anything related to the Beats. To me, looking at his work again decades later, he sounds just like himself—a characteristic blend of loudness, wit, shyness, pedantry, disgust (largely self-disgust) and gratitude.

What comes across now, especially in later poems like "Hortus Conclusus" (written to me), or the autobiographical "Epistle to Chester Kallman," is the gratitude and loyalty to friends. Near the end of his time in a new apartment on Dimocharous Street, across from the pines of Lykavettos, these friends included the cats he celebrated in another poem: "As the boys fade out the cats fade in / Jumping down from the tree, creeping under the partition, delicately walking the balcony railing, / Waiting for food, licking themselves, sleeping, spying, enjoying their state, / Modeling the being of God's creatures for a less satisfied one . . . What's the use? Expel the cats with a broomstick they return, / Hungry, weary, forgiving, distracting, / An opportunity for love."

Acknowledgements

"The Gorgon's Gaze:" *Ablemuse*, no 11, Summer 2012;

"Sylvia Plath into Greek:" *Times Literary Supplement (TLS)*, 9/14/2012;

"Talking to My Father:" *Southwest Review*, vol 99, no 2;

"Pages of Illustrations:" *Classics*, Textos Imprint, David Robert Books, 2007;

"Rachel Wetzsteon and Allusion:" *TLS*, 2/1/2013;

"Lucretius:" *At Length, vol 2*, 2012;

"On Judging a Poetry Contest:" *TLS*, 6/22/2012;

"Sam and Lycidas:" *Southwest Review*, vol 96, no 24, 2011;

"Snakes:" *TLS*, 11/16/2012;

"Invisibility:" *New England Review*, vol 32, no 1, 2011;

"Nothing's Mortal Enemy:" *Lancet*, vol 379, 6/9/2012;

"Attention:" *TLS*, 5/31/13;

"The Shadowy Shore:" *Literary Imagination*, vol 13, no 2, 2011;

"Pindar:" *TLS*, 2/17/2012;

"Q & A:" *Classics*, vol 24, no 2, 2003;

"Dreams:" *Bosque*, Fall 2013;

"Breitenbush:" *TLS*, 1/20/2012;

"Questions, Questions, Questions:" *Classics*, Textos Imprint, David Robert Books, 2007;

"Reading, Writing, Teaching, Time:" forthcoming in *Writer's Chronicle*;

"Alan Ansen:" *TLS*, 8/2/2013

Rachel Hadas's numerous books include a memoir, *Strange Relation*, (2011) and eleven books of poetry, most recently *The Golden Road* (2012). A new book of poems, *Questions in the Vestibule*, is forthcoming in 2016. She has also translated tragedies by Euripides and Seneca, coedited an anthology of Greek poetry in translation from Homer to the present, and edited an anthology of work by poets in a workshop she initiated at Gay Men's Health Crisis. A frequent reviewer and columnist for the Times Literary Supplement, Hadas lives in New York City with her husband and collaborator, artist Shalom Gorewitz. She is Board of Governors Professor of English at Rutgers University-Newark.